THE COMPASSIONATE
GOD

THE COMPASSIONATE GOD

C. S. SONG

ORBIS BOOKS
Maryknoll, New York 10545

The Catholic Foreign Mission Society of America (Maryknoll) recruits and trains people for overseas missionary service. Through Orbis Books Maryknoll aims to foster the international dialogue that is essential to mission. The books published, however, reflect the opinions of their authors and are not meant to represent the official position of the society.

Unless otherwise indicated, all biblical quotations have been taken from the New English Bible.

Manuscript editor: William E. Jerman

Library of Congress Cataloging in Publication Data

Song, Choan-Seng
  The compassionate God.

  Includes bibliographical references and index.
  1. Theology. 2. Religions. I. Title.
BR118.S66   230   81-16972
ISBN 0-88344-095-4 (pbk.)   AACR2

To Mei-Man, my wife,
who enables me to envision
the love and compassion of God
in a mirror more than dimly.

Contents

Chapter Twelve: Communion of Love   **242**

Notes   **263**

Index   **281**

Preface

Chuang Tzu (c. 399–295 B.C.) is a fascinating thinker in the history of Chinese thought. While drawing much on the wisdom of Lao Tzu, the enigmatic teacher of Tao, he went beyond Lao Tzu and developed his own brand of nature mysticism. In the book that bears his name, the *Chuang Tzu,* we find an amusing conversation between him and his friend Hui Tzu (c. 380–305 B.C.), a prominent logician who belonged to the School of Names (*Ming-chia*). Walking with Hui Tzu along the dam of the Hao River,

> Chuang Tzu said, "The white fish are swimming at ease. This is the happiness of the fish."
> "You are not fish," said Hui Tzu. "How do you know its happiness?"
> "You are not I," said Chuang Tzu. "How do you know that I do not know the happiness of the fish?"
> Hui Tzu said, "Of course I do not know, since I am not you. But you are not the fish, and it is perfectly clear that you do not know the happiness of the fish."
> "Let us get at the bottom of the matter," said Chuang Tzu. "When you asked how I knew the happiness of the fish, you already knew that I knew the happiness of the fish, but asked how. I knew it along the river."*

How do you know? This is the key question in this conversation. How does Chuang Tzu, a human being, know that a fish, a creature of a totally different kind, is happy? Is it not just a projection of Chuang Tzu's own state of mind? "You are not fish," says Hui Tzu. "How do you know its happiness?"

Chuang Tzu is not put off by Hui Tzu's question. He retorts: "You are not I. How do you know that I do not know the happiness of the fish?" Chuang Tzu beats Hui Tzu at his own game. Chuang Tzu refutes him by turning his own argument against him. Hui Tzu accuses Chuang Tzu of projecting his own feeling into the fish, but is Hui Tzu not doing the same thing in his comment on Chuang Tzu's observation of the fish? Is he not projecting his own thought into Chuang Tzu? But Chuang Tzu's counterargument only drives Hui Tzu to a more dogmatic position. He does admit that he is he and not Chuang Tzu, but still declares with a resolute tone: "It is perfectly clear that you do not know the happiness of the fish!" At this point, Chuang Tzu

---

*A Source Book in Chinese Philosophy, translated and compiled by Wing Tsit Chan (Princeton, N.J.: Princeton University Press, 1969), pp. 209–10.

must have realized that it is useless to continue the discussion. He says half to Hui Tzu and half to himself: "I knew it along the river."

The difference between Chuang Tzu and Hui Tzu is conspicuous. Chuang Tzu is able to bring his profound insight into the nature of things to bear on his daily encounters. He possesses vivid empathy for the living universe. The distance between him and the fish diminishes. He is able to see things not only from his own vantage point, but also from the vantage point of other creatures. He is keenly aware that he and the whole universe share a common destiny.

This thought-provoking conversation between Chuang Tzu and Hui Tzu is illuminating for Christian theology. Chuang Tzu and Hui Tzu seem to suggest two types of theology—a transpositional type and a nontranspositional type. For the theology of Hui Tzu type, what is experienced and interpreted from one particular aspect of life and faith cannot be transposed to other aspects of life and faith. Because human beings and fish have nothing in common—so Hui Tzu's argument goes—it is absurd to project human feeling into the fish. Likewise, what Christianity is and what it stands for culturally and spiritually are so different from other cultures and religions that it cannot project itself into them. Christianity is Christianity; it is not Hinduism or Buddhism. Communication between them in the human spirit is not possible. Traditional Christian theology has largely been this nontranspositional theology of the Hui Tzu type.

But there is another kind of theology, of the Chuang Tzu type. It is a theology capable of transposition. Just as Chuang Tzu puts himself in the position of the fish and perceives its state of being, this kind of theology crosses the boundaries of cultures, religions, and histories in order to have deeper contacts with the strange and mysterious ways and thoughts of God in creation. In the case of Chuang Tzu, his picture of the universe is not complete until he takes into his confidence other creatures that share with him this vast creation. Should not theology also be ready to transpose itself into unfamiliar situations to be confronted by the bewildering but gracious ways of God with all creation?

Such a theology calls for a sensitivity that can respond creatively to vibrations coming from the depth of the human spirit outside the familiar realm of everyday life. It requires from us largeness of heart and mind to realize the meanings that at first appear alien to our religious consciousness. Vast Asia, with its great diversity of religions and cultures, with its large number of nations and peoples whose spiritual heritages are at once their despair and their hope, invites us to such a theological adventure. What you read in this book is a humble but enthusiastic response to that invitation.

I want to thank those who have shared with me the pangs and joys of writing this book. I remember particularly Dr. Stanley Samartha, director of the subunit on Dialogue with People of Living Faiths and Ideologies, of the World Council of Churches, now retired in Bangalore, India, and Dr. Ans van der Bent, director of the library at the Ecumenical Center in Geneva.

They read portions of the manuscript and gave me much appreciated criticisms and comments. I regard it fortunate to have had the help of these fellow truthseekers to whom Asia is not merely a missiological concern, but more importantly a theological concern.

My sincere thanks also go to Dr. Ng Chiong-Hui (Shoki Coe), a most respected pioneer in theological education in Asia. Many of us second- and third-generation theologians in Asia are deeply indebted to him for his tirelessly promoting the contextualization of theology. He read parts of the manuscript and gave many insightful comments.

A special word of appreciation must be given to William E. Jerman, whose editorial work greatly improved the manuscript. His personal interest in Third World theological voices and his editorial skills are God's gifts to those of us who seek to put strange ideas, images, and symbols in the foreign language medium that is English.

To my wife, Mei-Man, and my daughters, Ju-Ping and Ju-Ying, who are my constant "theological" companions, teachers, and fellow students, I must express my profound gratitude. In this particular school of faith and theology, they enable me to gain flashes of insight into the mystery of life in God and in this world not contained in theological textbooks. I have learned from them as much as from our common Asian heritage that theology must be transpositional. Theology of transposition is an effort to respond to that mysterious and powerful bond of love with which the compassionate God creates, redeems, and re-creates a family and a human community.

Introduction

In the parlor of the garden house of Jadu Nath Malik at Daksineswar, Sri Ramakrishna (1836–1886), a Hindu priest at the Kali temple, had a vision of Christ. He was drawn into a deep trance by the picture of the Madonna and the Child hung on the wall with other pictures. As the story goes, "a deep regard for Christ and the Christian church filled his heart and opened to his eyes the vision of Christian devotees burning incense and candles before the figure of Jesus in the churches and offering unto him the eager outpourings of their hearts."

The vision captivated him completely for three days:

> On the fourth day, as he was walking in the Panchavati, he saw an extraordinary-looking person of serene aspect approaching him with his gaze intently fixed on him. He knew him at once to be a man of foreign extraction. He had beautiful large eyes, and though the nose was a little flat, it in no way marred the comeliness of his face. Sri Ramakrishna was charmed and wondered who he might be. Presently the figure drew near, and from the inmost recesses of Sri Ramakrishna's heart there went up the note, "There is the Christ who poured out his heart's blood for the redemption of mankind and suffered agonies for its sake. It is none else but that Master-Yogin Jesus, the embodiment of Love!"[1]

This was an unusual vision for a Hindu priest. Sri Ramakrishna was not, however, converted to Christianity. "Till the last moment of his life," writes Swami Nikhilananda, "he believed that Christ was an incarnation of God. But Christ for him was not the only incarnation; there were others—Buddha, for instance, and Krishna."[2]

Christ did not become the sole preoccupation of Sri Ramakrishna in his quest for religious truths. But the strange vision enabled him to discover another dimension of truth in his religious quest. Christ entered his mind and heart to take up a place beside Buddha and Krishna.

What is most striking in the story is that the vision did not just disappear. It came back to him later in an unusual person he met on the street in broad daylight. He knew at once that that person was not a native son. But strangely, he took notice of the stranger's nose—it was flat. The mention of

1

the nose was so casual that it could have been without much significance. But it proved otherwise. Apparently the sight of the stranger with a flat nose made a lasting impression on him, for it came up again in conversation with his disciples years later:

> Long after, in discussing Christ with his disciples who were able to speak English, he asked, "Well, you have read the Bible. Tell me what it says about the features of Christ. What did he look like?" They answered, "We have not seen this particularly mentioned anywhere in the Bible; but Jesus was born among the Jews, so he must have been fair, with large eyes and an aquiline nose." Sri Ramakrishna only remarked, "But I saw his nose was a little flat—who knows why." Not attaching much importance to those words at the time, the disciples, after the passing away of Sri Ramakrishna, heard that there were three extant descriptions of Christ's features, and one of these actually described him as flat-nosed![3]

Christ appeared to Sri Ramakrishna in all his strangeness. But there was something which softened his strangeness—his flat nose. The nose is the most prominent part of a person's face. The shape of the nose determines to a large degree the features of the face. But the nose does not merely determine a person's facial traits; it also reveals the shape and colors of a person's thoughts and emotions. It is a tale-telling nose that we have right in the center of our face.

It is small wonder that Sri Ramakrishna could not forget the flat nose of the strange person he had seen on the street. His disciples told him that in the Christian Bible there was no reference at all to Jesus' physical characteristics. They assured him, however, that since Jesus was of Jewish origin, he must have had a pointed nose. But Sri Ramakrishna was not convinced. He remarked somewhat in puzzlement: "But I saw his nose was a little flat." There is no way of knowing what had been going on in his mind during the years after his vision of Christ. Perhaps he was perturbed, unable to grasp the meaning of his strange encounter.

What interests us most in the story is that Christ appeared to Sri Ramakrishna as flat-nosed. We wonder why Christ did not appear to him as a full-fledged Semite, Anglo-Saxon, or Indo-European. "Flat-nosed" being a common description, rightly or wrongly, of people of Asian or, in particular, Mongolian extraction,[4] Christ with a flat nose must have bothered Sri Ramakrishna a great deal. Perhaps this is why he referred to it again later.

He might not have realized it, but it is possible that Christ in an Asian form must have begun to make way into his heart. This did not result in his "conversion" to Christianity, but Christ came to occupy in his mind the place of an *avatara* (divine incarnation) among other *avataras* such as Krishna and Buddha. This was as far as he could go as a Hindu priest, but we should not belittle the fact that Christ took hold of a Hindu heart in this unusual way. In the experience of Sri Ramakrishna we see the flat-nosed Christ cross the boundaries of races, religions, and cultures.

FROM THE POINT-NOSED TO THE FLAT-NOSED CHRIST

Transposition from the point-nosed Christ to the flat-nosed Christ—this may sound a little frivolous, but it in fact touches on the truth that Jesus Christ, to use St. Paul's words, "becomes everything to men [and women] of every sort" (1 Cor. 9:22). For nineteen centuries Christ was almost exclusively a point-nosed savior to the point-nosed persons of the world. And, apart from his point-nosedness, his other Semitic traits were gradually replaced by European ones. As Gayraud Wilmore, a black theologian in the United States, has pointed out:

In the history of Western painting the depiction of Christ evidences his progressive whitenization or bleaching with the object of changing him from a Semitic to an Aryan person. What must have been his dark hair was rendered as light-colored, his dark eyes as blue. It became a matter of importance that the incarnation of God be as far removed as possible from anything that would suggest darkness or blackness. . . . The Aryanization of Christ according to color symbolism commenced when White Europeans began to come into close contact with other races.[5]

For nearly two thousand years this "progressive whitenization" of Christ went on unhindered. Whiteness has played a decisive symbolic role for Christianity not only in the West but also in the rest of the world.

Incarnation of the Semitic Christ into western flesh seems complete. It is so complete that it has almost rendered incarnation in other skin colors sacrilegious. But a nagging question remains: how can the flat-nosed Asians and Africans truly recognize Christ and accept him as their kith and kin when he appears to them with a prominent pointed nose? But, because the Christian faith has to do with the truth, the truth that Christ is point-nosed, there cannot be a flat-nosed Christ, not to say a flat-nosed theology. There the matter should rest, and any further speculation about Christ's nose should cease.

The curiosity of flat-nosed humanity about Jesus' nose cannot, however, be suppressed. Although they do not quite know how to put their uneasiness into words, the point-nosed Christ continues to bother them. In the course of time, a kind of schizophrenia has developed in the mind of many thinking Asian Christians about Jesus' nose. This is most evident in Christian art in Asia. Richard W. Taylor says for instance of K.C.S. Paniker, the most creative Hindu painter in contemporary India: "It seems to me as if Paniker's Jesus looks more like his recollection of the Ramakrishna description. . . . I am not entirely clear about just what a flat nose looks like, but Paniker's noses of Jesus, while different from his other noses in paintings of the same period, do not look flat to me; but they look Semitic."[6] Apparently, Paniker was very much impressed by the flat-nosed Christ described by Sri Rama-krishna. But he had been under such strong influence of the point-nosed Christ that the flat-nosed Christ could not break into his canvas.

Another illustration of such a divided mind about Jesus' nose in Asia is "Creation" done by Twan Duchanee of Thailand.[7] In this painting, most of the figures, including Adam and Eve, are point-nosed, and their other physi-cal characteristics are decidedly western. But interestingly enough, at least five women in Thai attire are painted with the tip of their noses somewhat round, giving an impression of flatness. I do not think the painter did this consciously. It seems that by attiring these women in Thai dress, the painter, when he came to their noses, instinctively moved his brush in a round and not in a pointed fashion. This mixture of flat-nosed and point-nosed figures in the same painting is very instructive. Here the struggle between a flat-nosed culture and a point-nosed culture, though subdued, is evident.

It takes enormous willpower and uncanny imagination to come out a win-ner in such a struggle. Evidence of such willpower and imagination becomes increasingly visible in works of art on Christian themes by Asian artists. A number of examples can be mentioned. There is, for instance, the painting "Brown Madonna" by Galo Ocampo of the Philippines.[8] The beauty of this painting comes from its unpretentiousness, and its profundity from its sim-plicity. Apart from the halos above the heads of Mary and the Child, there is little to suggest a "religious" motif behind it, and yet it at once reminds one of the simple and homely stable in which the Savior was born. In fact the paint-ing conveys the ultimate meaning of the incarnation: God was in Christ be-coming one of us. Above all, both the Madonna and the Child are completely Asian, including their noses, which are pointedly flat. Transposition from the point-nosed Christ to the flat-nosed Christ has taken place.

The same is true of "The Madonna" by Unggun Permadi of Indonesia.[9] In this painting even the halos are gone. And what a stroke of genius for the painter to adorn the background of the painting with ordinary earthen jars! These jars link the Madonna and the Child to the real life of ordinary men and women. Golden halos definitely have no place in such a painting.

In Asian works of art it seems that God comes to the people in Christ in more and more recognizable forms. Asian artists are proving themselves to be creative both artistically and theologically. They have in many instances set themselves free from the ideas and forms of Christian art standardized by western painters. They have established a basic norm and criterion of Chris-tian art in Asia: the Word become flesh, not just in Bethlehem two thousand years ago, but *now* in *Asia*. This is not of course a denial of the heritage of the Christian faith. But in artistic creation in Asia insights into and experiences of the incarnation take different forms and expressions. The incarnation has become transposed in Asian Christian art. It is certain that in the days to come we shall see more works of art in Asia reflecting the power and grace of the incarnation through the Christ transposed from the West to Asia.

WHAT IS TRANSPOSITION?

The word "transposition" has cropped up more than once in our discussion, and it will be a key word in our continuing discourse. It is a "transpositional theology," in various aspects—history, Jesus Christ, community—that we hope to develop in our theological efforts. What then does transposition mean? In what sense do we intend to use it? How is it to be linked with theological concerns?

In what follows, we will address ourselves to these questions. We will begin with lexical meanings of the word "transposition." As we do this, we will try to see how the word can be used theologically to illuminate various shades and aspects of the incarnation. This may turn out to be an interesting adventure. Who knows? We may come across the God who, in the words of the writer of the Book of Revelation, "is making all things new" (21:5).

1. Transposition Is Shift in Space and Time

In *Webster's Third International Dictionary* several meanings are listed for the word "transposition." We select a few of them with particular significance for our discussion.[10]

First of all, transposition means change from one place or period of time to another place or period of time. It is equivalent to shift or removal. The sentence: His living quarters were transposed from the center of the city to the suburb, is an example. Transposition here means shift in space. As to shift in time, it can be illustrated by the following sentence: Social and economic analyses of Karl Marx in the nineteenth century have been transposed to theories and practices of social revolution in the twentieth century. Shift in time here is obvious. But we should note that the shift is not purely chronological. More importantly, it has to do with ideas and beliefs that change human understanding of life and the world.

Does this meaning of transposition have something to tell us theologically? Yes, it has. In the providence of God, the biblical world with its faith was transposed from Palestine to the Greco-Roman world and eventually to the rest of Europe and the West. The person who was chiefly instrumental in this transposition at its initial stage was St. Paul.

Jesus' immediate disciples did not forsee such a transposition. Even just before Jesus' ascension, they, according to Luke's account in the Acts of the Apostles, thought that the kingdom of God would be actualized without a transposition of the faith from Jerusalem to the rest of the world. They asked Jesus, perhaps with some impatience and apprehension: "Lord, is this the time when you are to establish once again the sovereignty of Israel?" Political sovereignty was still their main preoccupation. Jesus quickly discouraged this expectation and made it clear to them that transposition of the faith must take place first. He said: ". . . you will bear witness for me in Jerusalem, and all over Judaea and Samaria, and away to the ends of the earth" (Acts 1:6–8).

It was St. Paul who took up this missionary commission and carried the gospel, not to the ends of the earth as we understand it today, but to the Greek world and the Roman Empire, considered at that time the entire political and religio-cultural world. Through him transposition of the faith in Christ from the land of the Bible to the western world took place, ushering in the long era of western culture deeply influenced by the spirit of the gospel.

Has transposition of the Christian faith also taken place from the western world to the so-called Third World? It has. The story of this transposition is the story of the missionary expansion of the churches in the West during the last two centuries. In one sense, it has been a highly successful transposition. Here we may refer to some missiological forecast that gives us a picture of what the distribution of Christian population will look like in the future in comparison with the past.

According to Walbert Bühlmann, a Swiss Roman Catholic missiologist, "we are in the middle of a process of change as a result of which the Church, at home in the western world for almost 2,000 years, will, in a short time, have shifted its center of gravity into the Third World, where adherents will be much more numerous."[11] His prediction is based on the statistics in the Table of World Christian Population Concentrations.

Table of World Christian Population Concentrations

Christian population	1900	Year 1965	2000
Millions			
Europe, N. America	392	637	796
Asia, Africa, Oceania, S. America	67	370	1,118
Percentage of Total			
Europe, N. America	85%	63%	42%
Asia, Africa, Oceania, S. America	15%	37%	58%

In the year 1900 only 15 percent of the world Christian population was in the Third World; Europe and North America accounted for 85 percent. But by the year 2000 we shall be faced with a different picture: 58 percent in the Third World, 42 percent in Europe and North America.

Confronted with such a forecast, Christians in Europe and North America have some heart-searching questions to ask. What will the future of Christianity be in their own lands? How are they going to recapture the power of the gospel, especially in those countries where there is increasing indifference to the church? And how are they going to relate to Christians in the Third World who will surpass them in numerical strength?

Of course we must not elevate numbers and percentages into a form of cult. Numerical strength is important; it should not be minimized. But it should not make us forget the fact that transposition of the Christian faith to the Third World has largely been a second-hand and a third-hand transposition. A first-hand transposition is still to take place.

A journey from Israel to the Third World—and in our discussion here, from Israel to Asia—needs to be undertaken all over again. For one thing, the airplane ticket purchased for us to reach Asia from the biblical land was a nonnegotiable discount ticket. The journey was cut down to economy size. It had many intermediary stopovers. The most frustrating part of it was that the itinerary could not be altered. Everything had been decided in advance at a travel agency in the West. It is true that not everything in this economized flight was bad. There was much to see and learn on the way. We saw many impressive persons—with white vestments, rich miters, and imposing shepherds' staffs in Gothic churches and cathedrals. We met somewhat intimidating persons—with black robes and heavy beards in awesome basilicas and monasteries. We also found ourselves in the company of very learned persons who seemed to know Aristotle and Kant, as also the Christian Bible, inside out. On the whole, it was a rewarding journey. But it took too long and there were too many interruptions.

Despite excitement and wonder there were moments of frustration and fatigue. We were forever trying to catch up with churches with a wealth of traditions and learning. There seemed no end to this process of education. We did not know when we could graduate from this school of western Christianity. All this time, the *Analects* of Confucius was stacked away in the attic gathering dust. We did not quite know what to make of that beautiful classic *Dreams of the Red Chamber* that reveals untold woes and sorrows of the human heart in traditional Chinese families. We came dangerously close to disowning our own cultural heritage as having no useful meaning in the design of God's salvation.

Then it suddenly occurred to us that there must be a more direct flight from Israel to Asia, a flight which would have fewer stopovers and would allow changes of itinerary when occasions demand. To get on such a flight, we should not let others purchase the ticket for us. We must appear in person at the travel office and work out the itinerary with the travel agent. And most important of all, we must make sure that the ticket allows rerouting. A first-hand transposition of faith depends greatly on a negotiable ticket. The main purpose of a transpositional theology is to facilitate a journey from Israel to Asia with such a ticket. It searches ways in which God has not left the nations and peoples of Asia to the course of their own destruction.

2. Transposition Is Communication

The second meaning of transposition has to do with rendering into another language, style, or manner of expression. The key word here is translation. At international meetings where we are both impressed and dismayed by the babel of languages we at once realize the absolute necessity of translation. Without it exchange of information and discussion of ideas cannot take place; communication has to come to a standstill. This, in short, is mutual transposition of languages. Transposition as a spatio-temporal word now becomes a communication word. Transposition as communication is at the very heart of human activities that seek to transmit ideas, beliefs, and meanings in ways that will have communicative power.

How important this activity of transposition is in our daily life! Human relationships depend to a high degree on its success or failure, for life is made up of activities through words, signs, gestures, or movements of parts of the body; all these both disclose and conceal our inner thoughts and beliefs. This is especially true when cultural settings in which communication takes place change. Without transposition even simple gestures may lead to misunderstanding.

In India, for example, people shake their heads to express agreement or affirmation. In most other parts of the world, in contrast, shaking of the head means negation or disapproval. This is one of the basic facts you have to learn if you happen to be in India. You must realize that you are transposed to a culture in which agreement and disagreement are expressed differently. To give another example, in most parts of Asia, to beckon someone to come, you stretch out your arm with the palm of your hand facing downward. In the West it is just the opposite; you have to have the palm of your hand face upward with the fingers moving toward yourself. Contrasts such as these are numerous and good communication depends on how much attention we pay to them.

Intercultural and interpersonal transposition is therefore a prerequisite to human communication at all levels. But the sad reality in our society is that this very basic thing that makes our communication meaningful is often ignored or violated. In an authoritarian country, for instance, the power and authority of the ruler determine the contents and styles of communication. It is communication from the top down to the bottom. All communication systems are mobilized to serve the enforcement of the ideology of the ruling government and its policies. Authority to rule turns into authoritarianism, controlling the life and thought of people.

Revolt against authority is revolt against such authoritarianism. It is a socio-political upheaval in search of the kind of authority not built on ruthless power but on truth, not on violence but on love, not on coercion but on persuasion. Ideally this is what revolt of democratic forces against authoritarian power should be. Such a revolt exposes the fundamental weakness of authoritarianism: the authority that cannot be authenticated by truth loses its credibility; the authority discredited by love and justice forfeits its authenticity. The crisis of authoritarianism is the crisis of authenticity and credibility.

Theology is not immune from the crisis of authority. For a long time theology enjoyed extraterritorial privileges in the world of communication. Theologians did not have to worry too much about authentication of their theological statements. In fact authentication tended to be regarded as a sign of disbelief, the sin of the doubting Thomas.

There was, to be sure, some logicality in this. Because theology has to do with faith, and faith is more a matter of commitment than of argument, it does not have to be censored by the logic of human reason. As Anselm, the famous archbishop of Canterbury (c. 1033–1109), said: "I do not seek to understand that I may believe, but I believe that I may understand." Faith is the necessary foundation for our search for God. But the problem arises when this very foundation is called into question. Here theologians are in for trouble.

In modern western theology, it is Dietrich Bonhoeffer who, more than anyone else, questioned the faith-presupposition of theological statements. Writing from his prison cell in Tegel, he put it this way:

> And we cannot be honest unless we recognize that we have to live in the world *etsi deus non daretur*. And this is just what we recognize—before God! God himself compels us to recognize it. . . . God would have us know that we must live as persons who manage our lives without him. The God who is with us is the God who forsakes us (Mark 15:34). The God who lets us live in the world without the working hypothesis of God is the God before whom we stand continually. Before God and with God we live without God. God lets himself be pushed out of the world onto the cross. He is weak and powerless in the world, and that is precisely the way, the only way, in which he is with us and helps us.[12]

Bonhoeffer's language here is boldly paradoxical—"before God and with God we live without God"! What does this really mean?

Our attention is drawn to his stress on the weakness and powerlessness of God. He seems to be questioning the faith in a strong and mighty God who is ready at hand to save believers and rout unbelievers. For Bonhoeffer, confined to prison where no such ready succor was forthcoming, God was weak and powerless. This God was the God of the cross. This is why the language of faith has to change; theological discourse has to take a different style, and communication of the gospel has to choose a different manner of expression.

This shows that transposition of theology is more than just formal or linguistic. It has to do with the substance of the message which the church has to communicate. It requires theological discussion to shift to different subjects, to face new questions, and to discover alternative approaches. For Christians in Asia this could prove to be a colossal transposition of faith—it is a transposition from the world of biblical faith to the world of Asian cultures and religions.

3. Transposition Is Incarnation

Reflection on communication brings us to the center of our faith: the incarnation. Transposition is incarnation. This sounds a little abstruse. It seems very remote from our everyday life and from our historical experience. Actually it is not. The following episode from the history of modern China is an illustration of how important it is for transposition to take the form of incarnation.

At the turn of the century, a great controversy erupted in the cultural and intellectual scenes in China. It was the controversy between the traditionalists and the modernizers on the relationship between Chinese studies and western science, western democracy. Both traditionalists and modernizers were agreed that China should be liberated from humiliation and domination at the hands of foreign powers. It should struggle to free itself from its semi-colonial state and become a strong, autonomous nation.

At the heart of this contention was patriotism faced with the sorely disgraced conditions to which China had been reduced by foreign nations. Traditionalists and modernizers further agreed that western studies in some form could be enlisted to help China stand on its feet again.

But there was a sharp difference of view when it came to the question of the relation between Chinese studies and western science and technology. Before the May Fourth Movement in 1919, which exerted a profound impact on socio-political developments and cultural change in the ensuing decades, the predominant view was that of Chang Chih-tung, who in 1898 made the famous statement: "Chinese studies as the fundamental structure, Western studies for practical use" (*Chung-hsüeh wei t'i, Hsi-hsüeh wei yung*).

This seemed a neat solution to the otherwise insoluble problem. Behind it was the conviction that "in addition to learning scientific techniques, China should also model her laws and political institutions after those of the West," but that "Chinese philosophy, ethics and the fundamental principles of the traditional society. . . should not be changed."[13] This effort to make the best of the two worlds of the traditional China and the technologically advanced West did not work miracles. China continued to head for an almost inevitable disintegration through its own internal corruption and through mounting pressures from external forces.

This led to a revolution of new intellectuals during and after the period of the May Fourth Movement. The proponents of this "cultural revolution" maintained that "not only western scientific technology, laws and political institutions ought to be introduced, but also China's philosophy, ethics, natural science, social theories and institutions should be thoroughly reexamined and modeled after those of the West."[14] Westernization of China was their goal. Nothing short of this could, in their opinion, enable China to stand on a par with the powerful western nations. They had little sympathy for Chinese studies because they believed that it was studies of antiquated Chinese classics that had led China to the point where it was.

What went wrong in this celebrated controversy between Chinese studies and western science and democracy in that critical period in the history of modern China? Transposition of western studies into China was widely accepted as necessary for China to recover from its stagnation and helplessness. But in the question of how that transposition should be done the controversy got bogged down. There were those who asserted that introduction of western studies should in no way affect the spirit and substance of Chinese traditions, while others maintained that Chinese studies must be replaced entirely by western studies.

Both sides erred. They failed to see that no healthy cultural assimilation could take place without the two cultures becoming "incarnate" in each other. It is neither simply a matter of imitation nor a matter of uncritical fusion. It is a matter of an alien culture "become flesh" in a native culture. A metamorphosis must take place in the cultures concerned.

Does this story of cultural transposition in the history of modern China have something to tell us? I believe it has. The gospel, when transposed from its biblical world to other cultural worlds, undergoes change itself as well as causing these other worlds to change. The gospel is a very powerful thing. It not only changes human institutions and creates new values, but also changes the hearts of people. But it is not so powerful that it becomes change-proof. A change-proof gospel would be a very awkward thing. It could only fit into one situation. If it were rectangular in shape, it could not be fitted into a circle. If it came in white, it could never be in black or brown.

The wonderful thing about the gospel is that it could come in any shape and in any color. Furthermore, if it feels comfortable in a western suit, it is equally comfortable in an Indian sari or a Japanese kimono. St. Paul puts this marvelous changeability of the gospel in this way: "I have become everything in turn to men [and women] of every sort, so that in one way or another I may save some" (1 Cor. 9:22). To Jews he became a Jew; to the weak he became weak. If he were our contemporary, perhaps he would say: to Burmese I become like a Burmese; to the poor, I become poor.

In our mission and theology, we have constantly underestimated this enormous changeability of the gospel. But it is this changeability that makes the gospel what it is—the good news that God loves and saves people. How can the gospel not be changeable? The heart of the gospel is that God comes to the world. God becomes flesh in humanity, is incarnate in Jesus Christ and through him in us all. It must be a very bold God, for by becoming one of us, God risks becoming less than God and risks tasting the agony of God-forsakenness in Jesus on the cross. But because of the risk God has taken we are saved, and the world has a hope and a future.

In comparison, our mission and theology have often been very timid. We are afraid that we may lose sight of God in the temples of other believers. We are not sure whether we can hold onto God in the sea of humanity that crowds the streets of Hong Kong. But how can we serve this bold God with our timid faith? How can we follow this God whose frontiers are forever expanding when the frontiers of our theology are closed? How can we recognize this transposed God when our eyes remain fixed to the pre-transposed God? It is this God who changes, transposes, and becomes flesh in the human life that judges and redeems human beings and the world. The God of transposition is the God of incarnation. This is the faith that guides and leads our transpositional theology.

BLACK GOD OF BLACK CHRISTIANS

Black theology is an example of theology of transposition. This theology is set in the key of blackness. Blackness is the essence of the experience of faith for black Christians in the United States and in Africa. The catechism of the Church of the Living God founded by William Christian in Wrightsville, Arkansas, in 1889, is a splendid testimony to this. It has the following questions and answers:

Was Jesus a member of the black race?
Yes. Matthew 1.

How do you know?
Because he was in the line of Abraham and David the king.

Is this question sufficient proof that Christ came of the black generation?
Yes.

Why?
Because David said he became like a bottle in the smoke. Psalms 119:83.

What color was Job?
He was black. Job 30:30.

What color was Jeremiah?
He said he was black. Jeremiah 8:21.

Who was Moses' wife?
An Ethiopian (or black) woman. Numbers 12:1.

Should we make difference in people because they are black?
No. Jeremiah 13:23.

Why?
Because it is as natural to be black as the leopard to be spotted. Jeremiah 13:23.[15]

Is this not an outrageous exegesis? Surely it is. But for black Christians the Bible must become a black book before it can speak to them. The rules laid down somewhere outside their life experiences cannot bind them. They must open their Bible with their black hands, see it with their black eyes, read it aloud with their black mouths, and let the message of the gospel simmer into their black being.

But is blackness all that is important? Are black Christians making idolatry of blackness? If not, what does blackness mean in relation to the gospel? As James Cone, another prominent black theologian in the United States, puts it:

> Being black in America has very little to do with skin color. To be black means that your heart, your soul, your mind, and your body are where the dispossessed are. . . . Therefore, being reconciled to God does not mean that one's skin is physically black. It essentially depends on the color of your heart, soul, and mind.[16]

This is truly the heart of the matter. Black theologians seek to penetrate the human soul from the black skin. What they find there is the heart of the dispossessed, the poor, and the oppressed. It is there that they encounter the heart of the suffering God.

This is what makes black theology an ecumenical theology. Suffering is not the monopoly of black people. All the dispossessed, the poor, and the oppressed suffer, no matter what the color of their skin may be. They must reach the heart of the suffering God through their black skin; for them there is no other way. But when they reach there, they find themselves in the company of the dispossessed with all kinds of skin color. In the words of Wilmore, black theologians such as Cone

> open up the possibility of a Black theology which is neither Protestant nor Catholic, but the way Black people *think, feel* and *act* with the intensity of ultimate concern about their liberation from oppression and racism. Such a theology is rooted in the resistance of the historic Black church, but it extends beyond organized religion. It embraces also the attempt of Black secular and non-Christian groups to express verbally and to act the meanings and values of the Black experience in America and Africa.[17]

We need to bear this ecumenical possibility of black theology in mind as we seek to understand its implications for the church today.

Black theology is ecumenical in a twofold sense. It is ecumenical in that it transcends denominational and confessional boundaries. It is neither Catholic theology nor Protestant theology. It is *black* theology because it grows out of the experience of black Christians in the United States as an enslaved people. This painful experience of suffering has made denominational or confessional divisions utterly meaningless.

Further, black theology is ecumenical in the original sense of *oikoumene*—the world. Black theology crosses the boundary that has traditionally separated the church from the world. To use Wilmore's expression, it "embraces also the attempt of Black secular and non-Christian groups to express verbally and to act the meanings and values of the Black experience in America and Africa." How could a theology be more ecumenical! Here is a theology that does not pretend to speak and act universally on behalf of all humanity. It is rooted in black experience and remains faithful to it. And yet in doing just that it becomes ecumenical. Its voice is heard not only by black Christians but by black people outside the church. Even the world beyond the black community is rendered restless by its echoes.

IMAGE OF GOD IN WOMAN

Another ecumenical theology in the process of formation is feminist theology. The concerns of our sisters who make up half of humankind are not determined by confessional differences. And the tendency now is for these concerns to converge as global concerns. Women in many parts of the world are searching for a new image of woman in the human community dominated for centuries by patriarchal systems and male-centered social structures. Listen to this passionate poem, " . . . A Part of Me is Missing," by Anne Mc-Grew Bennett:

> Where is "me"
> a part of me is missing
> aborted—stillborn—
>   since that Garden time
>
>   yet without plan or warning
>   ever and ever again moving
>   deep within my body
>   and soul
>   a person "image of God"
>   WOMAN
>   comes grasping, grasping
>   for the breath of life
>   struggling to be born
>   and live—free
>
>   pushed back, covered over by
>   myriads of words—intoned word
>   *you are not man*
>   *you are woman*

created for a man's pleasure
and comfort
created to bear man-child
to rule you
created to bear woman-child
to be subject to man-child

Man-child, oh man-child
my father, husband, brothers, sons
do you feel a deep stirring,
rebellion
at the intoned word for you?
You are man, be big
be strong, powerful
never surrender: succeed
let no tears break through
be mind, not heart
heart is for the weak
be arrogant-aggressive

CRY, CRY BELOVED IMAGE
Who calls us both?[18]

cf,
Be whole .
Silverstein's The
missing
place

What a cry! What a plea! What a protest! If men still keep adamantly silent, "these very stones will shout aloud" (Luke 19:40, RSV)!

A voice crying out in passion for a new image of woman is also beginning to be heard in Asia. The language may not be so stirring and eloquent as that used by women in the West, but it unmistakably conveys the agony and aspiration hidden in the deeply troubled souls of Asian women in search of the image of God in them.

Agnes Loyall from India, for instance, says: "The Asian Woman must be liberated from oppression and ignorance, but she must be liberated from the traditional image of herself as *only* a mother, a wife and homemaker. She can be all these plus more. She can be an active, productive, contributing member of society in her own right as an equal of man in any profession or in any field. She must believe in this new image of herself and strive in every way to project this image."[19]

This is a call not only to Asian women but also, and perhaps more importantly, to Asian men. A new image of Asian woman must be the outcome of cooperation between Asian women *and* Asian men. And what is more, a new image of Asian woman will surely bring into being a new image of Asian man.

Reading these words, whether from East or from West, one feels as if a volcano is erupting, the earth is shaking, and an abyss is breaking open. For what we—women and men—are going through today is the pain of a new creation, the birthpangs of a new image of woman and a new image of man in

God. A revolution of a most radical kind is in the making here. The world that has treated women as the property of men is a wrong-side-up world. This wrong-side-up world must be turned right side up. The coming into existence of a right-side-up world is revolution; it is creation. Feminist theology is a theological effort to serve this new creation.

The consequences of this kind of theology can be far-reaching. Take the idea of God, for example. God in traditional theology is masculine from head to toe. Such a God is a personification of male power, authority, and even brutality. In the name of this masculine God, theology has justified the sub-servient position of women in church and in society; the church has refused to ordain women to the priesthood and perpetuated the hierarchical structures centered in male power.

Feminist theology has launched a frontal assault on this very citadel of traditional male theology. In the place of this masculine God, it begins to disclose to us a God with tender love and quiet passion, a God who is strong in weakness, firm in softness, approachable and embracing in the fullness of beauty. Is this the same God whom most male theologians have written about from, say, Thomas Aquinas to Karl Barth? I am not quite sure. Transposition of a masculine God to a God who is experienced in the love and passion of women is bound to bring about change in our perception of God in the human community.

CENTRISM: A ROADBLOCK TO TRANSPOSITION

With these explanations and illustrations, I hope I have made clear what transpositional theology is about. Theology has already become transposed from its home in the West to other parts of the world. Latin American theology of liberation is a notable example of such theological transposition. Together with black theology and feminist theology, theology of liberation has been making its great impact widely felt in various churches and theological circles.

This raises for us as Christians in Asia the question of what theology will look like when transposed to Asia. We must further ask: how should such a transposed theology go about its task? What should be its main concerns? How should it relate itself to the histories, cultures and religions where it has found a new home? And what are the roadblocks that stand in its way?

One of the roadblocks that creates a major problem for transpositional theology in Asia is the centrism with which traditional theology is accustomed to view the history of Israel and the history of Christianity. This roadblock of centrism must be removed so that the road may be cleared for theological traffic in Asia.

As I see it, the job set before us here can be carried out in three steps. The first step is to locate the forces in the Old Testament that draw Israel out of its centrism and set it in relation to other nations. The second step is to see how Jesus fought to liberate his own people from ethno-religious centrism. These two steps will, I hope, clear the road for the third step: our journey into movements of nations and peoples in Asia that may give us some clues to the ways of God in that vast portion of the world outside the Judeo-Christian traditions.

These three steps give the basic structure to this book. In the first part we propose to look at the faith of the Old Testament in the perspective of *disruption-dispersion*. In the second part we want to see how Jesus' disciples came to perceive their master quite differently after the traumatic experience of *the great disruption* of the cross and resurrection. Finally, in the third part we shall see, under the theme of *transposition*, that some historical and human experiences in Asia disclose to us the heart of God in agony and compassion.

Part I

DISRUPTION – DISPERSION

For my thoughts are not your thoughts,
   and your ways are not my ways.
   This is the very word of the Lord.
For as the heavens are higher than the earth,
   so are my ways higher than your ways
   and my thoughts than your thoughts.
                              [Is. 55:8–9]

CHAPTER ONE

Many Peoples,
Many Languages

"Once upon a time all the world spoke a single language and used the same words," so begins the story of the Tower of Babel in Genesis 11. What an ingenious way for the ancient storytellers to conclude the primeval history! The picture that the first eleven chapters of the Book of Genesis have painted—God creating the universe and contending with various forces of chaos—is anything but a picture of peace and order. No sooner had unruly elements been brought under control than tragedies of cosmic magnitude erupted one after the other.

First came the fall. It affected the creation in a most profound way. It was not just the fall of Adam and Eve from the grace of God through their disobedience. It was the fall of the whole of humanity into the power of decay and death.

From then on the primeval history was marked by titanic efforts to stem further erosion of the created order. The struggle was not altogether successful. The comfort and consolation which Adam and Eve found in the family bond of love was soon marred by the blood of fratricide. Out of jealousy and anger Cain slew his own brother Able. The monstrosity of Cain's murderous act was expressed in the words God said to him: "Hark! your brother's blood that has been shed is crying out to me from the ground" (Gen. 4:10). Once the precedent of shedding blood was set, one breach after another was introduced into human society. Lamech retaliated with murder for the wound he had received from a young man (4:23–24).

The goodness God had seen in the created world was in serious jeopardy. It was as if the movement of the creation had come to a halt. A halt did come. It came in the form of a cosmic flood which enveloped the universe, threatening it with total destruction. A new beginning had to be made.

God's covenant with Noah marked the beginning of a new history for the creation and for humankind. Written into the covenant was God's promise not to destroy humankind and to ensure the orderly movements of nature. "Never again will I curse the ground because of man," God announced, "however evil his inclinations may be from his youth upwards. I will never again kill every living creature, as I have just done. While the earth lasts, seedtime and harvest, cold and heat, summer and winter, day and night, shall never cease" (8:21–22). With these divine blessings one would expect that the primeval history would have ended on a happy note.

But the ancient storytellers denied the primeval history a happy ending. A divine-human "comedy" it was not going to be. The primeval history had to conclude with the story of the Tower of Babel that caused disruption and dispersion of the human community. History did not seem to be carried forward as uninterrupted continuity.

THE TOWER OF BABEL REVISITED

In the minds of Christians, the tower has always stood as a witness to human pride. Gerhard von Rad, a German Old Testament theologian, for instance, suggests that "the unity and linguistic familiarity of mankind" was the presupposition of the story. He goes on to say that "the unity as a sign of their valiant self-reliance, the tower as a sign of their will to fame" is a kind of "concealed Titanism."[1] Von Rad further observes that the tower was "an aetiological saga" that "seeks to explain why there are so many nations and languages" and also "intends to explain the name of Babel."[2] He may be right in all this, but the theme of disrupted continuity should not escape our attention.

The construction of the tower was motivated perhaps not so much by titanism as by fear of dispersion that might bring disruption to the community. The crucial statement in the story, it seems, is: "or we shall be dispersed all over the earth," rather than the one preceding it: "and make a name for ourselves" (11:4). Fear of dispersion is fear of disruption.

The Tower of Babel, whatever else it might have been, was insurance against fear of disruption. It is something like the monuments that can be seen everywhere, from ancient times to the present day. A monument is symbolic of continuity. Its purpose is to preserve in human memory what time may otherwise obliterate. It seeks to extend into the future what has been achieved. It is meant to be a memorial that links the past, the present and the future into one continuous flow of time. A monument is a sign of an eternal present.

And of course a monument bears the name of the person to be remembered. There is a Chinese proverb to the effect that a tiger leaves its skin behind, and human beings leave their names. A name is a person. It is what a person is and stands for. Obliteration of the name after death is obliteration of the person that goes with that name. For this reason alone death is something to be dreaded. As is said in the Book of Job, in death one's "memory vanishes from the face of the earth" and one "leaves no name in the world"

(18:17). Death destroys life and disrupts history. A monument is a human device against the terror of death.

But God challenges the human effort to resist dispersion and to maintain continuity. History must, from time to time, be disrupted and people must be dispersed into all parts of the world. Did not God say to the human creature when the work of creation was completed: "Be fruitful and increase, fill the earth and subdue it, rule over the fish in the sea, the birds of heaven and every living thing that moves upon the earth" (Gen. 1:28)? The construction of the tower is resistance to the divine command to "fill the earth." It must therefore be disrupted.

Very few exegetes have understood dispersion to the world not as God's punishment for human pride but as fulfillment of God's command. S. R. Driver, a British Semitist, seems a rare exception. He makes a rather discerning remark saying that the story of the Tower of Babel "shows how the distribution of mankind into nations, and diversity of languages, are elements in His [God's] providential plan for the development and progress of humanity."[3] In a very interesting way, the end of the primeval history—the Tower of Babel in Genesis 11—gets linked up with the beginning of the primeval history—the creation in Genesis 1 and 2.

Our point is that the building of the Tower of Babel should not be regarded merely as an audacious attempt on the part of human beings to storm and seize the kingdom of Heaven by force. What impels the builders of the tower is perhaps not so much pride or arrogance as fear—fear of dispersion into many nations, fear of losing their immediate coherence and security. To get around "God's providential plan" to fill the earth with a multiplicity of nations that speak a diversity of languages, they must have put their heads together and come up with the idea of building a tower that would make "one people/one language" a *fait accompli.*

Their attempt must be frustrated. They must be dispersed to form many nations and speak different languages—the plan ordained by God. Disruption of the tower construction is to implement God's purpose for "the development and progress of humanity."

THE TOWER OF BABEL QUESTIONS *HEILSGESCHICHTE*

Understood in this way, the story of the Tower of Babel raises questions as to the meaning of Israel and the Christian church held in traditional theology. Biblically and theologically, it has been firmly held that Israel and the church form one continuous history representing God's plan of salvation. The emphasis falls on continuity.

Various paradigms are used to explain this continuity. The most common paradigm is that of prediction and fulfillment. What is predicted in the Old Testament concerning God's salvation is fulfilled in the New. Another paradigm is derived from the concept of covenant. The (old) covenant God had made with the patriarchs and through them with the whole of Israel developed into the (new) covenant through which God enters into a new relationship with Christian believers in the church. Whatever paradigm is used, it is stressed that God's salvation continues from Israel to the Christian church.

Can we not detect in this a kind of Tower of Babel mentality? The difference is that the ancient tower builders sought to consolidate their coherence *in space,* trying to reach as high as heaven, whereas theologians of the Christian church affirm the unity and continuity of Israel and the church *in time* as the most essential part of God's salvation, reaching into the *eschaton*—the end of time.

This, of course, is the theological position summed up in the concept of *Heilsgeschichte* (salvation history). Viewed from the standpoint of *Heilsgeschichte,* world history has no direct link with God's salvation until it is touched by *Heilsgeschichte* and brought into the sphere of its influence..

Oscar Cullmann, a Swiss New Testament theologian, has advanced a view typifying such a perception of God's salvation in his famous book *Christ and Time*.[4] He identifies what he calls "redemptive history" as a "slender" line[5] between the old creation and the new creation with Christ at the midpoint under the principle of "progressive reduction and progressive advance." He further calls this slender line of redemptive history "the Christ line," since Christ is "the Mediator of the Creation—Christ, God's Suffering Servant as the One who fulfills the election of Israel—Christ the Lord, ruling in the present—Christ the returning Son of Man as the One who completes the entire process and is the Mediator of the new creation."[6]

There is something in this theology of *Heilsgeschichte* that does not quite tally with the historical experience of those people outside the Christian church, and Cullmann seems aware of it. He explains his view of redemptive history as "a paradox of Christian universalism" which combines "the most extreme concentration and the widest universalism."[7] But is this a true paradox? One is not so sure, for in his theological scheme he firmly maintains "the difference between the narrower redemptive history as it unfolds in the Church, and the universal process."[8] How do the narrower redemptive history and the universal process come into interplay? How are they related? Are there mutual interactions between them?

We look in vain in Cullmann for new answers to such questions. Typically, this is what he tells us:

> . . . the entire redemptive history unfolds in two movements: the one proceeds from the many to the One; this is the Old Covenant. The other proceeds from the One to the many; this is the New Testament. At the very midpoint stands the expiatory deed of the death and resurrection of Christ. . . . Common to both movements is the fact that they are carried out according to the principle of election and representation. This principle then is decisive also for the present phase of development, which proceeds from the midpoint. The Church on earth, in which the Body of Christ is represented, plays in the New Testament

conception a central role for the redemption of all mankind and thereby for the entire creation.[9]

Election and representation of Israel and the church, and in Cullmann's view, especially the church, on behalf of all humankind! These two concepts have been the two solid pillars supporting the claims of Christianity to uniqueness among other faiths and religions. The main actors on the stage of redemptive history are Israel and the church. Other nations and other peoples fade into the background. They have to be represented by Israel and the church because they have not been elected. The line of redemptive history is a straight one. It does not bend. Nor does it deviate from its predetermined course.

A STRAIGHT-LINE GOD AND A STRAIGHT-LINE THEOLOGY

Obviously, this kind of straight-line theology will not do. To be sure, it has many advantages. It is logical, for one thing. Just as B must follow A in the alphabetical order, straight-line theology captures God's saving activity in a very orderly fashion. In Cullmann's case, it is the principle of "progressive reduction and progressive advance" that is decisive. This logical order of salvation allows no interference: creation, the fall, the election of Israel, Jesus Christ, the church as the new Israel and final fulfillment, follow one after the other. The line of salvation history cannot be diverted or disrupted.

I seriously doubt that a straight line can express the immense complexity of God's saving activity in the world. A straight line simplifies. It cuts off irregularities. It straightens out knotty problems. It geometrizes everything it touches, even God and what God does. It is such a handy tool for theologians to have. We have to concede that a straight line is one of the most basic and essential units for science and technology. Without it skyscrapers would collapse and human adventures into space would be forced to stop.

Modern culture of science and technology is a straight-line culture. Should a straight line refuse to cooperate and begin to bend, turn or wiggle, horrible consequences would surely follow. A metropolis might turn into a heap of ruins. Human habitats would change their shape out of recognition. If we had to single out the important items that make life not only livable but enjoyable, the straight line would have to be high on our list. We are all children of this straight-line culture, for better or for worse.

But when it comes to a quite complex matter such as God's dealings with humankind, we begin to wonder if the straight-line concept can still work. In fact, to turn God into a straight-line God is to caricature God. Love, for example, is a most simple and yet most powerful thing. It brings lives into being, sustains them, nourishes and enriches them. Love is the Word through which God comes to us and we to God. "God is love," says 1 John 4:8.

It is plain to everyone that love is not a geometrical concept. It cannot be measured by a ruler. It cannot be weighed on a balance. It cannot be straightened out by a line. And least of all is it a straight line. Love is round, not straight. It does not penetrate space like a straight line, but fills it and saturates it. It is not a linear but a concentrical movement. It is not analytical but synthetic. It is not judgmental but embracing. A straight line judges, punishes, eliminates, but love forgives, caresses, embraces, and includes. God is not a straight line but love. The straight-line God of *Heilsgeschichte* is a hard, stern God who has predetermined who are to be saved and who are to be condemned.

Furthermore, the straight-line God must be a monotonous and unamusing God. The God of traditional theology wears a long face, sitting grimly on the theological throne. Even saints and angels surrounding the divine throne are caught in this grim and pensive mood of the straight-line God. It is seldom that one comes across a laughing God, a laughing Christ, a laughing saint, or a laughing angel in the Christian church—Catholic, Orthodox, or Protestant.

Laughter has long departed from the church and theology. Once stepping into the church, we Christians leave our laughter behind. We forget to laugh in the church. We think it not proper to laugh during worship service. Even when singing: "Hosanna, in the highest!" we are straight-faced and solemn. We are too conscious of the straight-line God staring at us from a pedestal high above. He seems ready to catch any sign of mischievousness in us. But a religion that has done away with laughter can be a dangerous thing. It can stir up witch-hunting. It can resort to burning heretics at the stake. It can start a religious war, exterminating unbelievers and infidels. Should we not then pray: O God, give us back our laughter!

Laughter breaks monotony of life. It interrupts conversation. It disrupts a story. It brings relief to a life that has become burdensome. It creates new rhythms to enliven the stagnant spirit. That is why there must be

> a time to weep *and* a time to laugh;
> a time for mourning *and* a time for dancing [Ecc. 3:4].

A laughing and dancing God—this is the God of most Asians and Africans outside the Christian church. This God laughs with them as well as weeps with them. This God dances with them as well as mourns with them. Worshiping this God, Africans "beat their drums, play musical instruments, dance and rejoice. Religious singing is often accompanied by clapping and dancing, which express people's feelings of joy, sorrow or thanksgiving."[10] How different this is from Christian worship in a solemn assembly!

Worship is celebration of God who gives life and takes it away. Celebration must be a noisy thing. Clapping, singing, and dancing—such noisy assembly is a communion of God and people in deep ecstasy. Worship in ancient Israel must have been very much like this. Listen to Psalm 47, for instance: "Clap your hands, all you nations; acclaim our God with shouts of joy" (47:1).

As we Christians gather together to worship God, why have we ceased to clap our hands? Why do we refrain from dancing? Why do we scrupulously avoid laughing, even smiling? We want to keep the whole worship service as a unity. We fear that clapping and dancing will disturb it. From start to finish, worship must flow like still, clear water, allowing no muddying by shouts and laughter. But we pay a heavy price for this, for excitement has left Christian worship. Worship service moves from one stage to the next in an orderly manner. The straight-line God must be honored through straight-line worship service. A straight line runs through the Christian church, its history, its life and liturgy. The main task of the church is to see to it that a predetermined scenario is faithfully reproduced along the straight-line course of *Heilsgeschichte.*

FALSE AND GENUINE PARADOXES

History is much more than a linear movement. The linear view of history is very much a product of the scientific mode of thinking. It is an explanation of history based on scientific convenience. A modern, scientifically inclined person cannot tolerate imprecision of thought, deviation from a verifiable worldview, and mysterious lacunas that resist penetration by scientific reason. Being beneficiaries of this scientific and technological age, theologians too tend to measure life and history with theological precision. All that does not conform to the continuous linear movement of *Heilsgeschichte* is anomalous and perhaps ungodly. From this traditional theological standpoint, it is difficult to develop a theology of history that could shed some light on the question of how God is also at work in the life and history of persons outside Israel and the Christian church.

Christian theology of history has thus had a tendency to be an incommunicable kind of theology. Christopher Dawson, an English theologian of history, says for example:

> . . . it is very difficult, perhaps even impossible, to explain the Christian view of history to a non-Christian, since it is necessary to accept the Christian faith in order to understand the Christian view of history, and those who reject the idea of a divine revelation are necessarily obliged to reject the Christian view of history as well. And even those who are prepared to accept in theory the principle of divine revelation—of the manifestation of a religious truth which surpasses human reason—may still find it hard to face the enormous paradoxes of Christianity.[11]

If what Dawson says is true, then understanding among people of different cultures and religions is an illusion. For if the Christian view of history cannot be understood by persons outside the Christian church, how can Christians expect to understand the Hindu view of history or the Buddhist view of history? We are confronted with a wall of silence before which we feel helpless and impotent. All that is left for us to do is either to withdraw into our isolation or to resort to proselytism.

Dawson also refers to "the enormous paradoxes of Christianity" to explain why the Christian view of history cannot be understood by others. But are his paradoxes genuine or false paradoxes? What he calls the paradoxes of Christianity may be by-products of cultures and histories in which the churches in the West have developed.

As to the supreme paradox of the incarnation, it is something else. By incarnation we mean God being present in Jesus Christ, and through him being with us, sharing our burden and giving us hope and life. This is the paradox of God in the midst of the world, weaving with us human beings the fabric of life and history. If this is the paradox of our faith, why can it not be understood by other persons? It cannot be understood by others when Christian interpretation of it does not touch the fabric of their life, when it does not take into account the fact that God has as much to do with their history. Here is a whole new frontier for Christian theology of history. Biblically and theologically, we need to find ways to approach that frontier.

The truth of the matter seems to be that God moves in all directions—forward of course, but also backward, upward, and also downward, inward, and also outward, and perhaps diagonally too. The Spirit of God and the human spirit are not confined to one particular direction. They interact in all sorts of ways. The outcome of such divine-human interaction is history. There is much, much more in such history than is dreamed of in our theology. How are we to grapple with such history? Looking at the history of Israel from a different angle, we might gain a partial answer.

ISRAEL IN DISRUPTION AND DISPERSION

Israel and the nations—this is not a new subject, but new insights into their relations should not be ruled out completely. Each nation has a center—political, military, cultural, or spiritual. But this center does not remain immobile. It is in fact like an epicenter from which tremors of the angry Mother-earth spread in concentric circles farther and farther out into distance.

In the ancient Mediterranean world, Greek culture under Alexander the Great spread far and wide, even to the Indus Valley in the northwest of the subcontinent of India. In modern times, western military and political powers made their impact felt all over the world, forcefully pushing open the doors of those nations in the Third World and colonizing them. And for the last two centuries or so, ethnocentric culture of China has been implanted not only in southeast Asia, but also in the West, particularly in North America, through the Chinese in the diaspora. Nations come and go, leaving behind them traces of mutual contacts and impacts and creating new relationships and interactions. Israel has to be seen in this great movement of nations and peoples.

To change our imagery to describe this truly astonishing phenomenon of history created out of divine impacts and human responses, just imagine you are standing on a beach. The vast ocean glistening under the sun is spread before your eyes. In the far distance, you see the waters of the ocean and the high canopy of heaven merge into a thin line of horizon that marks, it seems, the limit of the otherwise limitless universe. And then you see, hear, and feel waves rising out of the abyss of the sea, traveling a great distance from that horizon, battling their way to the shore. With sounds alternating between agonizing murmurs and seductive serenades, the waves finally win the shore. But they recede as quickly as they came, leaving behind them water to simmer into the sand on the beach and become one with it. In this perpetual ebb and flow, waves and sand remain separate only to casual observers. For more attentive minds, the arriving waves become amalgamated with the beach sand, and the beach sand is carried away by the receding waves to be dispersed into the ocean. Waves in the sand and sand in the waves—waves and sand come into each other and live in each other. And together waves and sand form a part of the mysterious and living universe. Israel and the nations—are they not like waves and sand, distinct yet interdependent?

1. Abraham Uprooted

The call of Abraham in Genesis 12 seems a good place to begin our fresh inquiry into the relations of Israel and the nations. The historical nature of the story of the call does not concern us here. What is important is that in their traditions the people of Israel regarded Abraham as the patriarch par excellence, for it is with him that Israel emerged out of its obscurity and entered the stage of history.

In telling the story, either in oral or written form, the storytellers saw to it that the call of their revered patriarch was filled with dramatic intensity. According to their belief, Abraham's departure from his home in Upper Mesopotamia for a totally unknown land was not motivated by an adventurous spirit like great explorers such as Christopher Columbus, but was a response to God's call. The dangerous journey was undertaken under the irresistible urging of the divine spirit. That is why God's call came to Abraham in the form of a promise: "I will make you into a great nation!" (12:2).

This was the faith of Israel looking back upon the beginning of its history. At the time when the story of Abraham's call was put down in writing, Israel had already achieved stability and secured its place among the nations and tribes of Canaan under King David and King Solomon. Israel was already a great nation. How could a small beginning such as Abraham's journey from his ancestral home have developed into the glory of such a great nation? God must have granted Abraham a promise and this was the fulfillment of that promise.

Furthermore, it must have been this promise that had given the will, courage, and strength to the small confederacy of Hebrew tribes to gain a foothold in Palestine, the land of many powerful nations. There was thus a "messianic" echo in the promise. And as it turned out, it was a "messianic" promise such as this that justified their bloody and brutal exchanges with

Canaanite peoples. We can almost say that if the ancient people of Israel had not had such a "messianic" promise, they would have had to invent one.

The hagiographic nature of the history of Israel aside, the story of the call of Abraham seems to fit the pattern of disruption-dispersion after the model of the Tower of Babel. In the words of one commentator: "The divine address begins with the command to abandon radically all natural roots. The most general tie, that with the 'land,' is named first, then follow, narrowing step by step, the bonds of the clan, i.e., the more distant relatives and the immediate family. These three terms indicate that God knows the difficulties of these separations; Abraham is simply to leave everything behind and entrust himself to God's guidance."[12] "Uprootedness" seems one of the ways in which God brings peoples and nations into close proximity with one another.

We cannot fail to recognize a remarkable correspondence here between the Tower of Babel and the call of Abraham. As has been mentioned, the disruption of tower construction and the dispersion of one people into many nations and languages are in keeping with God's design for the creation. Abraham's call to leave his land and his clan is a part of this design. Had he refused to accept the call and remained rooted in his ancestral home, a new nation called Israel would not have come into existence, and the history of the ancient Near East would have taken quite a different turn. But most important of all, the drama of Israel and the nations struggling to find their places in God's design of salvation would have lost its intensity and excitement, had Abraham decided to let his natural ties of land and clan dictate his future. For him this was a great risk of faith, but without that risk God's design for creation and salvation would have been seriously impaired.

2. The Migrating God

The grandeur of history begins in this way, with the pain of disruption and dispersion. This is an important clue to our theological understanding of the history that includes Israel and the nations. At the heart of this history is God as the force that disrupts and disperses. But God does not stay put in one place, directing movements of peoples from a secure fortress. God not only calls people to move and migrate; God also moves and migrates. It is a moving and migrating God. God cannot be pinned down and become localized. Psalm 139 is a beautiful and magnificent ode to this migrating God:

> If I climb up to heaven, thou art there;
> if I make my bed in Sheol, again I find thee.
> If I take my flight to the frontiers of morning
>   or dwell at the limit of the western sea,
> even there thy hand will meet me
>   and thy right hand will hold me fast [Ps. 139:8–10].

This is a theology of migration at its best. God is at the head of the migration column and the leader of the migrating people. Migration begins with God's order and continues under God's direction. This faith in the migrating God ought to help expand the frontiers of our historical experience. It should help extend the boundary of our faith into the faiths that create different cultures and histories. For God is the power that moves peoples and nations. We encounter here a dynamic God.

Later, this theology of migration developed into the theology of the ark of God. The migrating God takes now the form of the ark. The ark comes to stand for God who moves, sustains, advances, and migrates. The compilers of the Book of Numbers put the movement of the ark vividly in this way:

> Then they moved off from the mountain of the Lord and journeyed for three days, and the Ark of the Covenant of the Lord kept a day's journey ahead of them to find them a place to rest. The cloud of the Lord hung over them by day when they moved camp. Whenever the Ark began to move, Moses said: "Up, Lord, and may thy enemies be scattered and those that hate thee flee before thee." When it halted, he said, "Rest, Lord of the countless thousands of Israel" [Num. 10:33–36].

God is not looked upon as a spectator in this great movement of the people of Israel. God marched in front of them and "kept a day's journey ahead of them." This is God's active involvement in movements of people. The migrating God becomes "incarnate" in the migrating people. God is the grace and power that sustains the painful and dangerous life of migration. That is why the ark of God is the ark of hope.

3. Exodus: A Convulsive Disruption-Dispersion

This pattern of disruption and dispersion, first disclosed in the story of the Tower of Babel and later demonstrated at the beginning of the patriarchal history, comes to an explosive expression in the exodus. For a long time Egypt was a hospitable home to the families of the patriarchs driven out of Canaan by famines. But the time finally came when the Egyptians began treating their once welcome guests as hated slaves. This love and hate relationship between Israel and Egypt was a long and complex one lasting until the present day.

For the Hebrew tribes struggling under harsh conditions in Egypt, the exodus was a disruption of the long enslavement and a dispersion into the lands beyond the Red Sea. It was a convulsive disruption and dispersion accompanied by terrible disasters and death. But it marked a great milestone in the history of the formation of the Hebrew nation. Through this tumultuous event of disruption and dispersion, the enslaved people emerged from their enslavement and stood on the threshold of a new history with other nations. Abraham, their first patriarch, headed westward from Mesopotamia in search of the promised land. Now they had to march northward from Egypt to gain that same land.

How many cycles of disruption-dispersion they had to go through in the wilderness to reach the banks of the River Jordan! It was a long stretch of time—forty years—filled with dramas of hopes and setbacks that the wandering people learned to interpret in faith. Their successes and failures, their victories and defeats, were viewed and accepted as the manifestation of the will of Yahweh, their God.

4. Covenant and Israel's Political Theology

The axis of interpretation is of course the Sinai covenant. The words of God addressed to Moses on Mount Sinai make this clear:

> You have seen with your own eyes what I did to Egypt, and how I have carried you on eagles' wings and brought you here to me. If only you will now listen to me and keep my covenant, then out of all peoples you shall become my special possession; for the whole earth is mine. You shall be my kingdom of priests, my holy nation. These are the words you shall speak to the Israelites [Ex. 19:4–6].

For the tribes confronted with the enormous difficulty of forming into one unified nation surrounded by hostile nations and peoples, the Sinai covenant served as their rallying point. The covenant was to hold together the loosely organized tribes through thick and thin during the seemingly endless journey of pain and suffering after the flight from Egypt.

The theology of migration mentioned earlier now took a more definite form in the theology of the covenant. And what came to loom large in it almost out of proportion was the consciousness of being chosen by God to become a special nation among all nations. "Out of all peoples you shall become my special possession," Moses heard God saying to him. Israel was to be God's "holy nation." For the people striving toward a political existence, faith in God's election constituted the essence of the covenant.

To use modern jargon, this is what may be called "political theology of the covenant." And at the heart of this political theology was the divine election. In this way, the social and political aspirations of Israel found their spiritual ground in the covenant of election. The God who moves and migrates among the nations began to be drawn into a particular theological framework built on the historical experience of a particular nation.

But as it turned out, the people of Israel overplayed this political theology of the covenant of election. In the name of the covenant of election, they built a racial and religious community that was closed to outsiders. God's election became their right over against other peoples, and not God's grace that could as well be granted to other nations.

As we shall see, it was the prophets who challenged such a narrow and exclusive theology of election and tried to help their compatriots see how God was working in the wider arena of world history. Indeed, what we now know as racism is a tragic version of such misguided and distorted theology of the covenant of election. Initially, there seems to be no relationship between election as an experience of God's free grace and election as a justification for apartheid, the form of white racism practiced in South Africa. But by turning grace into a claim, one achieves the feat of turning theology of election into theology of apartheid.

Apart from social and political apartheid, there is what we may call spiritual apartheid, which separates adherents of different faiths one from the other on the question of salvation. For Christians in particular, there has always been a tendency to turn salvation into a point of contention. Some Christians believe that the line that divides the elected and the nonelected, the saved and the nonsaved, is absolutely clear. They are in no doubt that God's salvation works solely within the Christian community.

The missionary outreach of the churches in the West very much reflected this exclusive claim to salvation. "Most of the missionaries of the past centuries," says Michael Collins Reilly, an American Jesuit missionary to the Philippines for some ten years, "took an extremely negative stance regarding the possibility of salvation outside the Church. Compassion for lost souls drove them to superhuman efforts to tell others of Christ and to baptize millions."[13]

One cannot help wondering why God's salvation should become such a contentious subject. Basically, salvation means that God heals divisions that exist within us human beings and in the human community. It means that God restores health and wholeness to us as individuals, as community, as nations. It means that reconciliation between God and humanity is God's decisive act in freedom and grace. God has not given monopoly right of salvation to anyone. In fact the whole point of salvation is lost if such monopoly right is institutionalized into God's salvation.

Salvation becomes a point of contention only when it gets out of God's hand, when it becomes a part of a religious institution. Salvation loses its saving power when it has to be protected from all sides by papal bulls and theological orthodoxy. If God's salvation is such a fragile thing, how can it save us "tough" sinners? If it is such a delicate ware, how can it do its work in the rough and tumble of this world? If it does not have self-authenticating power, how can it be a healing power to those who suffer in body and in spirit? And if it divides people into different religious categories of saved and nonsaved, favored and nonfavored, elected and nonelected, how can it be the source of unity for a badly divided humanity?

It is important to know that the prophets in the Old Testament realized the danger of putting the covenant of election to ideological and political use. According to Walther Eichrodt, a German Old Testament theologian:

It remains . . . a surprising phenomenon that throughout the period when the *classical prophets* were drastically criticizing the popular religion of Israel, the covenant concept should recede into the background. It is certainly an exaggeration to consider . . . that generally speaking the prophets before Jeremiah knew nothing of a covenant relationship

of God with Israel. It is after all a fact that Hosea speaks twice of the
b*rit* that Israel has broken (6:7; 8:1). Nevertheless it is worth noting
that even for him the emphasis is not the covenant concept, but that he
makes use of other categories to describe the religious relationship.[14]

Why this sparse use of the concept of covenant? Is not the history of Israel a
covenant history? Is not its relation with God a very special kind of covenant
relation? Is it not because of the covenant that Israel stands out as a distinct
and almost a *sui generis* nation among the nations? And have we not, in
Christian theology, extended the concept of covenant to the Christian church
and interpreted its history as the history of the new covenant? Have we as
Christians not regarded ourselves—as the people of this new covenant—quite
different from other peoples? Has not the covenant concept played a decisive
role in our understanding of the church, sacraments, salvation, and our relation with the followers of other faiths?

But, if Eichrodt's observation is correct, we must ask why the covenant
concept receded into the background in the prophets' criticism of the prevailing religion of Israel. It may be that the prophets, such as Amos, Hosea, or
Isaiah, must have realized that covenant understood as election was doing
Israel a disservice. They saw that covenant had become the basis on which the
people made claims on God's favor. Covenant gained with God's grace became the people's right. It became something that the people could use to
bargain with God for special favors. They thought they could exploit God
with the covenant. They could even blackmail God with it. In their religious
use of it, covenant ceased to be a strong expression of God's love; for them it
was the disclosure of God's weakness. In the covenant they thought they
seized God's weak spot.

This is the danger of a covenant faith or a covenant religion. The prophets
could no longer identify with a covenant of election misused as a theological
justification for Israel's political existence among the nations. A basic change
must be brought about. For Amos the covenant of election gave way to justice; for Hosea it was replaced by love; and for Isaiah renewal of faith and
trust in God were far more important than ostentatious expressions of religiosity.

Indeed, ostentation is one of the great temptations for religion. Perhaps we
human beings are by nature ostentatious or exhibitionistic. Even love and
justice can succumb to our ostentatious and exhibitionistic urge. Jesus knows
well the danger of religious exhibitionism. He has little liking for it; he points
out that it is no better than religious hypocrisy. It must be with some sarcasm
that he refers to the religious leaders of his day who "love to say their prayers
standing up in synagogues and at the street corners for everyone to see them."
Then he tells his disciples what they should do when they pray: "When you
pray, go into a room by yourself, shut the door, and pray to your Father who
is there in the secret place" (Mt. 6:5–6). The God of Jesus seems a shy God
who avoids public places and luxurious religious meetings.

But our religion, our prayers, expressions of our Christian love and charity, become all too public and ostentatious. In our urge to act, to express ourselves, to let others hear us, we cannot hear unspoken words in our neighbors' hearts; we fail to read the silently agonizing minds of our friends, and we have no patience with those people of other faiths sitting in quiet but earnest contemplation on the meaning of life and the world. Are we as Christians closer to the shy God of Jesus than they are? Perhaps this is not an important question. But we must ask ourselves: how do we serve this unostentatious suffering God with our rich religious ceremonies, our elaborate truth claims, and theological systems? This is the question that the classical prophets in ancient Israel had to ask. This is also the question we must take seriously. For it may be that as we are busy expressing ourselves, calling the attention of others to ourselves, and asserting our truth over against other truths, we have missed the God "who is there in the secret place."

Christian theology has made this God in the secret place too transparent; it has made us see through God. This of course is our theological illusion. The task of theology today, especially for those of us Christians in Asia, is to meet and encounter the God who may be there in "the secret places" of nations and peoples, their religions and cultures.

5. *Israel Uprooted and Dispersed*

As the prophets predicted, the official theology of the covenant of election did not stand the test of time. The history of the divided kingdoms of Israel and Judah was anything but a peaceful one. It was a history ridden with court intrigues, bloody coups, and invasions by foreign powers. This in fact was not much different from the political history of the nations in East or West, ancient or modern. In their political experience, Israel and Judah shared with all other nations the agony as well as the glory of power. By becoming an organized political institution, they became subjected to the law of history that governs the rise and fall of nations and empires.

Although the rise to power of a nation or empire is often unpredictable, its decline and fall is predictable. In 722 B.C. the northern kingdom of Israel came to its end and its people were deported to Assyria. Israel disappeared from the historical map of the ancient Near East.

The prophet Isaiah must have watched all this in great anguish. Despite his ardent hope for the tide of history to turn in Israel's favor, Isaiah had to admit that the fate of Israel was irreversible. He vented his passion and anguish partly in chagrin and partly in relief when he called Sennacherib, the king of Assyria, "the rod which God wields in anger":

> The Assyrian! He is the rod that I wield in my anger,
> and the staff of my wrath is in his hand.
> I send him against a godless nation,
> I bid him march against a people who rouse my wrath,
>   to spoil and plunder at will
> and trample them down like mud in the streets [Is. 10:5–6].[15]

The kingdom of Israel was disrupted and its people were dispersed to the land of their conqueror. A new kind of exodus began.

A little more than a century later, the course of the Judean kingdom ran out. The land of Judah was devastated by the powerful Nebuchadnezzar, the king of Babylon, and Jerusalem fell to his hand in 587 B.C. Zedekiah, the hapless king of Judah, was forced to witness the murder of his sons before he was blinded and taken into captivity in Babylon. The house of David came to a violent end and its people set out on a sad exodus into the land of their victor. With his characteristically melancholy eloquence Jeremiah the prophet sang a dirge, paying his last tribute to his beloved Zion:

> Hark, hark, lamentation is heard in Zion:
>   How fearful is our ruin! How great our shame!
> We have left our lands, our houses have been pulled down.
>   Listen, you women, to the words of the Lord,
>   that your ears may catch what he says.
>   Teach your daughters the lament,
>   let them teach one another this dirge:
>   Death has climbed in through our windows,
>   it has entered our palaces,
>   it sweeps off the children in the open air
>   and drives young men from the streets [Jer. 9:19–21].

What could one say about the history of the people that had started out in such high hopes but ended so miserably? How should one judge a nation that, despite a strong sense of divine election, was not spared the fate of other nations? The Deuteronomic historians who traced this strange history of a chosen people in the Books of Joshua, Judges, Samuel, and Kings, as well as in the Book of Deuteronomy, sadly concluded: all this happened because the Israelites had sinned against their God Yahweh.[16]

With the exile the Jews experienced a most radical kind of disruption and dispersion in their history, comparable to the call of Abraham and the exodus. The historical continuity fostered and maintained by the theology of the Davidic kingdom was broken.

The devastation inflicted by the victorious enemies was enormous. "As archeological evidence eloquently testifies," writes John Bright, an American Old Testament scholar, "all, or virtually all, of the fortified towns in the Shephelah and central hill country (i.e., in Judah proper) were razed to the ground, in most cases not to be rebuilt for many years to come (cf. Lam. 2:2,5). . . . The population of the land was drained away. Aside from those deported to Babylon, thousands must have died in battle or of starvation and disease (cf. Lam. 2:11f, 19–21, 4:9f), some—and surely more than we know of (2 Kings 25:18–27)—had been executed, while others (cf. Jer. ch. 42f) had fled for their lives."[17] Jerusalem, the reality and symbol of Jewish national unity and piety, its religious power spent, could not rise again from the shambles of destruction and death. It fell on the exiles representing "the cream of their country's political, ecclesiastical, and intellectual leadership"[18] to make a new beginning in a foreign land.

The exile caused the spiritual gravity of Israel to shift decisively from its cultic concentration in Jerusalem to diversified manifestations among the nations. This seems to contradict the belief held both by Jews and Christians that the restoration of the Jerusalem temple was the fulfillment of God's promise after the destruction of the Jewish nation. The circumstances of the restoration of the temple was in fact much more modest and controversial than many of us think. According to John Bright,

> . . . the rank and file of the restoration community, including the clergy, were not distinguished by any great zeal for cultic and ceremonial regularity. On the contrary, as rebukes administered them by their prophets (e.g., Malachi) indicate, most of them were exceedingly lax in such matters—and continued to be even after Nehemiah had given the community assured political status. The new Israel wanted desperately something to draw it together and give it a distinctive identity; and this was supplied by Ezra through the law book that he brought from Babylon and, with authority from the Persian court, imposed on the community in solemn covenant. . . . This meant . . . a fundamental redefinition of the term "Israel." Israel would no longer be a national entity, nor one coterminous with the descendants of the Israelite tribes or the inhabitants of the old national territory, nor even a community of those who in some way acknowledged Yahweh as God and offered him worship. From now on, Israel would be viewed (as in the theology of the Chronicler) as that remnant of Judah which had rallied around the law. He would be a member of Israel (i.e., a Jew) who assumed the burden of that law.[19]

It is this religion of the law that was later opposed by Jesus. And it was this same religion that was to send him to the cross.

What needs to be emphasized in contrast is that in the exile the paradigm of disruption and dispersion proves once again its dynamic character. The prophet who had the deepest insight into this dynamic of disruption and dispersion as part of God's design for the nations is Jeremiah. In him is combined political realism with farsighted spirituality. He counseled surrender to the Babylonian invaders as the latter were assaulting the fortified gates of Jerusalem.

In his letter to the exiles written shortly after 598 B.C., when the first group of Judeans was deported to Babylon, Jeremiah prepared them for the life of dispersion. He wrote to them:

> Build houses and live in them; plant gardens and eat their produce. Marry wives and beget sons and daughters. . . . Seek the welfare of any

city to which I have carried you off, and pray to the Lord for it; on its welfare your welfare will depend [Jer. 29:4-7].

A narrow-minded nationalist hardened by religious centrism could not have written such words. The eyes of Jeremiah, however, were opened to God's design for the nations as well as for his own nation. No one single nation could contain the power of God that moves history. And with the fall of the kingdom of Judah, Jeremiah must have sensed that history-moving power of God operating in Babylon.

The course now is set for the Jews to be dispersed throughout the world. It began in Babylon. It has continued for more than two thousand years. It has been a long way from the Tower of Babel and from the call of Abraham. Through disruption and dispersion, nations and peoples are led to realize that God is greater than one's own nation, one's own religion and culture.

One particular nation alone, even that of Israel and Judah, cannot make a total picture of what God is doing in the world. It is only after Assyria and Babylon were brought into the arena of history that a more complete picture of God's design for the world began to appear. In the same way, one particular culture alone, even that which is called Christian culture, cannot reveal the entirety of God's thoughts for the world. Until Hindu culture or Confucian culture is consulted, the God of Christians remains a partial God.

So the exiled Jews must seek the peace and welfare of the nations. They must learn how their God is at work in the whole of history. With the exile they have embarked on the course to gain that knowledge and experience. From that time onward, the Jews in the diaspora played a prominent role in western civilization. They have been astonishingly creative in many areas of life and work in the countries of their adoption. As Berdyaev, an exiled Russian theologian, has remarked: "Within Christian history itself there is a constant interaction of the Hebrew and Hellenic principles which together make up the main sources of our culture."[20]

NO PROXY THEOLOGY

This has been an all too brief discussion that does not quite do justice to the long and complex history of Israel, but it at least shows us that the growth of the faith of Israel has to be seen in the light of the dynamic of disruption and dispersion that moves history. We have identified three great cycles of disruption and dispersion, with each cycle giving rise to a theology reflecting how the people of Israel apprehended their God and their relations with the surrounding world.

The first of these cycles begins with Abraham's response to God's call to leave his home and set out on a journey to the promised land. This is the framework within which theology of migration comes into being. The next cycle comes from the complex of the exodus and the conquest. Here it is the theology of the covenant that becomes fundamental to the alliance of the

Hebrew tribes trying to establish themselves in the midst of hostile nations. As we have seen, this theology of the covenant later becomes a state ideology serving as the religious foundation for the construction of the Israelite kingdom. The third cycle is that of the exile that carries the people of Israel and Judah to Assyria and Babylon, to the region where Abraham's migration originated. This is perhaps more than just a coincidence, for it is in the land of their origin that they have to realize that they share their roots with other nations. In the territory of foreign nations they must wrestle with the theology of the nations.

Through the experience of the exile and captivity, the Jews must have learned that there is no such thing as theology of history by proxy. The Assyrians and the Babylonians are not related to God through them. These foreign nations seem to have a direct access to God. They are not absent after all before the court of God's counsel. They are not represented by the Jewish people as their proxy. They can speak for themselves before God; they can even be sent by God as an instrument in the punishment of Israel and Judah. What an upsetting thought this is! To think of these other nations in terms of proxy will no longer do.

Christian theology of history has, to a large extent, been a proxy theology. The church has inherited the mantle of representation from Israel and takes upon itself the task of representing other people before God. It seldom occurs to it that people outside it may be quite capable of speaking for themselves and giving account of themselves before God. In its theology it leaves little room for them to come directly to the throne of God's grace. In its systems of beliefs and theology they gain salvation only through the proxy of the church.

Why has the Christian church come to acquire this proxy character? Why has Christian theology taken upon itself to speak on behalf of all humanity almost totally from the religious and cultural standpoints of Christianity? One of the reasons seems to be the concept of "uniqueness" that Christians freely use to describe the faith and life of the Christian church. The history of Israel is a unique history. The history of Christianity is also a unique history. Being unique, the history of the Judeo-Christian traditions is a history set apart from all other histories. The history represented by Israel and the Christian church becomes "sacred" history. It is a unique history that illuminates other histories but is in no need of illumination by them.

In this way, Christian theology has created a vacuum between the history of Israel-church and the history of other nations and peoples. This has led to the concept of *Heilsgeschichte* in which those outside the sacred history of Israel and the church have only marginal importance. Obviously this kind of theology hardly enables us to see how a nation not included in the Judeo-Christian tradition fares in God's creating and redeeming work for the world.

But there are clues in the Christian Bible that God's design of salvation for creation goes far beyond traditional Christian theology of history. These clues seem to show us that God takes each and every nation as seriously as God does Israel and the Christian community. In Israel and the church God's design of salvation is revealed with great intensity. But that intensive self-disclosure of God there does not exclude God's other self-disclosures in other forms in other places with varied degrees of intensity. For Christians in the Third World who become more and more exposed to their own history and culture, these biblical clues take on great significance. In the following chapters we will continue our search for these biblical clues to prepare our way for a theology of transposition.

CHAPTER TWO

God of All Nations

The faith of Israel grows, expands, and changes. It is tested by its own history. It is also tested by the history of other nations. In this double test the enlightened minds of Israel realize that world history is not a totally alien history. True, world history of which Israel is only a small part appears to be alien, inhospitable, and hostile. But is the power working in the depth of that alien history not the power that has given birth to the history of Israel? Is the life vibrating in the fabric of that history not the life lived and shared by Israel?

The power of world history is the power that comes from God. The life of the nations is the life that is created and nourished by God. This is truly a great, and for that matter shocking, discovery. The seers and thinkers of Israel can only express it in bewilderment and amazement. They perhaps do not fully understand what they have perceived on the wider horizon of history. But they realize that here they are in touch with something much greater than their national and cultural experience; it is something they cannot comprehend without enlarging their faith. They are confronted with a reality that can be grasped only by the religious mind that is capable of great imagination.

Apocalyptic language and imagery must have taken its rise in the faith that seeks to express in perplexity and in anticipation the mystery of God's activity in human history. Conventional language and imagery of faith are poor instruments when it comes to a matter that goes beyond one's immediate sphere of existence. They can be useful up to a point, but once that point is passed they fail miserably. New language must be invented and new imagery must be found.

This is the exciting thing about apocalyptic language and imagery. In pursuit of God's mystery, they break language conventions and trespass the boundary of familiar imagery. They thus enable us to follow God into history with apocalyptic expectation for a new heaven and a new earth. In apocalyptic language and imagery we experience liberation from the shackles of history and are empowered to work toward a new historical reality that bears the

41

marks of God's love and justice. The Book of Daniel is an example of such an apocalyptic experiment.

APOCALYPTIC HISTORY IN THE BOOK OF DANIEL

History and apocalypse are therefore twin brother and sister. They are conceived in the same womb, nourished by the same life-force, grow and mature in the close company of each other. History without apocalyptic meaning is an endlessly boring tale, a monotonous tabulation of dates, places, and happenings that will not stir up anybody's imagination except that of an archivist. It may be like a mummy from an ancient Egyptian tomb or an embalmed body in a modern mausoleum, although having all the appearance of a human being, yet lacking in one vital thing—life.

On the other hand, apocalypse without history has little historical significance. It becomes a pure human fantasy that has no relation to reality. It is nothing more than the human mind taking refuge in the realm of unreality. History and apocalypse must therefore be closely joined together and we should not tear them asunder, for history is made alive by its apocalyptic meaning and apocalypse bears meaning for our lives when it becomes related to history. We can say that history and apocalypse together disclose the meaning of the past, enlighten our present perplexities, and direct our paths to the future. Hence the coining of the phrase "apocalyptic history."[1]

The Book of Daniel is such an apocalyptic history. It contains a wealth of historical data. At the very outset, the editor-redactor[2] of the Book sets the stage of his narratives in a specific historical context saying: "In the third year of the reign of Jehoiakim king of Judah, Nebuchadnezzar king of Babylon came to Jerusalem and laid siege to it" (1:1). This would be the year 600 B.C. The account of Nebuchadnezzar's dream and its interpretation are preceded by a chronological reference: "In the second year of his reign Nebuchadnezzar had dreams" (2:1). The year mentioned here would be 603 B.C.

The visions Daniel saw concerning the vicissitudes of Babylon and Persia all have fixed dates. It is recorded in Daniel 7:1, for example, as follows: "In the first year of Belshazzar king of Babylon, as Daniel lay on his bed, dreams and visions came into his head." The year here would be 554 B.C., the third year of the reign of Belshazzar's father Nabonidus, when the rule of Babylon was officially entrusted to him.

To give another example, Daniel's reflection on the meaning of the contemporary history of his own nation is placed "in the first year of the reign of Darius son of Ahasuerus (a Mede by birth, who was appointed to the king's business over the kingdom of the Chaldaeans)" (9:1). Darius was the successor to Belshazzar as king of Babylon and the date here is probably 538 B.C.

These and many other instances underline the fact that apocalyptic visions are closely related to historical situations that reformers seek to change and transform. Apocalyptic visions, besides being historically oriented, are ethico-political. They are the indictment, in covert language and imagery, of the prevailing social and political conditions and provide the spiritual impetus for people to work for change and struggle for a better future. This again shows that apocalypse can be one of the powerful forces that bring about radical change in a people's orientation toward life and the world.

It has to be added that not all references to historical data in the Book of Daniel are accurate. Nebuchadnezzar's march to Jerusalem is said to have taken place in the third year of the reign of Jehoiakim (1:1), that is, in 606 B.C., as mentioned above. But actually it was not until 598 B.C., when Nebuchadnezzar waged a punitive campaign against Judah to punish king Jehoiakim, who had rebelled against Babylon. Further, identifying Darius the Mede as son of Ahasuerus in Daniel 9:1 is clearly wrong, for King Xerxes (Greek form of the Persian name Khashayarsha, namely the Hebrew Ahasuerus) of Persia was the son, and not the father, of King Darius I of Persia. Nor is it correct to place, as in the second chapter of Daniel, the Median Empire as the second empire between the Babylonian and the Persian. In fact the Median Empire was a little older than the neo-Babylonian Empire and was destroyed more than a decade earlier than the latter.

These are some obvious historical inaccuracies. But they do not diminish the apocalyptico-historical importance of the Book of Daniel. They do not alter the fact that the apocalyptic concerns in the book are historical concerns, that apocalyptic messages are historical messages. These concerns and messages are directed to those people caught in difficulties and tribulations at certain junctures of their history.

Norman Porteous, a British Old Testament scholar, is therefore right in saying:

In a book of this kind, in which stories are told primarily for their inspirational value, what concerns us chiefly is the historical reality of the contemporary situation, which the author has in view and in which he and his first readers were involved, rather than the question as to what degree of historicity can be assigned to the *dramatis personae* who occupy the stage in the literary invention and to the events which are narrated of them. . . . What first claims our attention is the relevance of the stories to the day for which they were recorded.[3]

REIGN OF TERROR UNDER ANTIOCHUS EPIPHANES

What then are the inspirational values which the Book of Daniel sought to inculcate in its readers? What is the direct purpose behind the apocalyptic interpretation of history set forth in it? What is its main historical focus?

These questions cannot be answered without looking into the date of the Book of Daniel. And this question of date in turn is related to the composite character of the book. Because it is not our task here to discuss various theories advanced by scholars in their historico-critical study of the book, let us just refer to the conclusion most of them have reached. It is generally agreed that the main burden of the Book of Daniel has to do with the persecution of the Jews in the reign of Antiochus IV Epiphanes. That puts the compilation of the book sometime between 168 and 165 B.C.

In the notorious Antiochus the Jews saw the personification of the arch-devil. His "senseless extremes prompted Polybius to speak of Antiochus as *epimanes* (Greek for 'madman') rather than as *(theos) epiphanes,* '(God) manifest,' a title he assumed in 169 B.C."[4] He looted temples and shrines, enforced total Hellenization, and massacred the Jews who refused to comply with his despotic whims. He descended on the God-fearing Jews as a chief instrument of Satan determined to exterminate them and their faith.

To feel the anguish of spirit that the Book of Daniel tries in vain to contain, we only need recall some monstrous acts Antiochus committed against Jews to crush their spirit, their faith, and their culture.

> In 167 B.C. Antiochus sent Appollonius, commander of the Mysians, to crush Jerusalem once and for all. The wily general entered the city, pretending to be peaceful. Then on the Sabbath, aware that the orthodox Jews would not take up arms to defend themselves, he attacked, slaughtering a large number of men; women and children he enslaved. He put fire to the city and tore down its walls. He built the Akra as a citadel for the Syrian troops and Jewish Hellenizers (mostly wealthy priests and nobles). Now determined to abolish the practice of the Jewish religion completely in his domain, Antiochus strictly forbade the Jews to live according to their ancestral customs. He abolished Jewish sacrifices and festivals, prohibited circumcision and observance of the Sabbath and dietary laws, built pagan shrines and altars, and ordered swine and other unclean animals to be sacrificed. Antiochus perpetrated the ultimate villainy in December 167 when he erected in the Jerusalem temple a statue of the bearded Olympian Zeus, placing it on an altar built right over the great altar of holocausts. This disgraceful shrine is "the appalling abomination" of Daniel 8:13, 9:27, 11:31 and 12:11. . . .[5]

Who can blame the Jews if they saw in this "appalling abomination" an eschatological battle fought between the forces of good and evil? Who can accuse them of escapism if they longed for an eternal life beyond this world of atrocity? How can anyone charge them with religious fantasy if they believed in the eventual intervention of God? As a fitting finale to such an eschatological hope in the midst of danger and desperation, the Book of Daniel gives us a vivid vision of the future:

> At that moment Michael shall appear,
>> Michael the great captain,
>> who stands guard over your fellow-countrymen;
>> and there will be a time of distress

> such as has never been
> since they became a nation till that moment.
> But at that moment your people will be delivered,
> everyone who is written in the book:
> many of those who sleep in the dust of the earth will wake,
> some to everlasting life
> and some to the reproach of eternal abhorrence.
> The wise leaders shall shine like the bright vault of heaven,
> and those who have guided the people in the true path
> shall be like the stars for ever and ever [12:1–4].

Here we see how history and apocalypse intersect. With faith we learn how to relate history to apocalypse and apocalypse to history. It is on apocalyptic history that we build our faith. Faith projects the here and now into eternity, but it also seeks eternity in the present. Through apocalyptic literature such as Daniel and Revelation we are trained to look at ourselves, our own nation, and the family of nations and peoples through the eyes of eternity.

GOD OF THE NATIONS IN SECOND ISAIAH

The immediate historical focus in the Book of Daniel is the tragic confrontation between the Jews and Antiochus Epiphanes in the mid-second century B.C. This does not mean, however, that all the stories in the book are written in the same period. This is particularly true insofar as the stories in Daniel 1–6 are concerned. "It is probable," writes James Barr, another British Old Testament scholar, that these stories "originated in the Diaspora under the Persian or early Greek empires, for their original setting is not a situation of persecution of Judaism by the state."[6] This puts the date of these stories between the sixth and the fourth centuries B.C.

This at once places some of the stories in Daniel 1–6 in the proximity of the great works such as those by Second Isaiah (Is. 40–55) in the exilic period. This is an important point to remember, for it implies that the theology of history in the Book of Daniel must have reflected the kind of transpositional theology that had taken shape in the land of captivity. What is the essence of this transpositional theology? How does it view the relationship between Israel and the nations? What does it say about God and the nations? Second Isaiah has some pointed answers for questions such as these. We will therefore explore a little the transpositional theology of Second Isaiah in order to understand better the background of the theology of history that provides the basis for the Book of Daniel.

What we see, to begin with, in Second Isaiah is a towering monument to the human spirit liberated from its national and religious limitations under the irresistible Spirit of God. The memory of Jerusalem, the ruined holy city, is still painfully vivid in the mind of the pious Jews. It is so firmly rooted in their being that no passage of time seems able to obliterate it. A people in captivity is not only a captive to its victorious enemy but also a prisoner to its own past. It lives in the past and finds no viable substitutes for it in the present or in the future. Indulgence in the past becomes an excuse for not accepting the present and working for a new future. Restoration of what is gone becomes its main preoccupation.

To these prisoners of the past the prophet Second Isaiah has some startlingly fresh message to proclaim. "Comfort, comfort my people—it is the voice of God" (Is. 40:1). His fellow captive Jews must have heard the message half in disbelief and half in astonishment. How could the God who allowed the destruction of their nation to happen and had them exiled to the enemy's land be a God who comforts? Do we not have a very uncomforting God? How could one again find the source of comfort in such a God? The prophet must have read such questions in the minds of his hearers, for it is no secret that "Zion says, 'The Lord has forsaken me; my God has forgotten me' " (49:14).

A people forsaken and forgotten by God—this is what they consider themselves to be. They have not only been dispossessed of their land, they are also dispossessed of their God. They have become a *land-less* people. But what is worse, they have also become a *God-less* people. They used to be full of God. From early morning till late at night, and even while they slept, they were filled with God. They never neglected to worship God and bring God gifts and sacrifices at the temple—the place most filled with God. They were the God-filled people in the God-filled land. But all this has changed. They now feel God-forsaken and God-forgotten.

But the prophet tells them something quite different, and he tells it in a vivid imagery of a mother and her child: "Can a woman forget the infant of her breast, or a living mother the child of her womb? Even these forget, yet I will not forget you" (49:15). What a strong and enduring memory God has! The memory that binds a mother to her child is strong, sacred, and inviolable. The child is part of the mother. It is her flesh and blood. The pain of her child tearing itself away from her at birth makes her remember it all the more. To be a mother is to remember her child.

What a comfort and what a relief it must have been then to be told that God's memory of the people is even stronger and more enduring than that of a mother! God's memory of them is absolute; it is categorical. If God forgets them, God ceases to be God. Because God will never cease to be God, the people will never cease to exist in God's memory. The God of memory is the God of hope. Insofar as God remembers them despite their national and personal tragedies, they have a hope and a future.

But just when the Jews in exile might indulge in self-congratulation, Second Isaiah reveals a startling thought: their future is not going to be simply and purely an extension of their past history. God has in mind a future that is much greater than their national future. God's memory is not limited to the memory of them. It covers the whole creation. It embraces all humanity. For God is the God

> who created the skies and stretched them out,
> who fashioned the earth and all that grows in it,
> who gave birth to its people,
>> the breath of life to all who walk upon it [42:5].

A truly universal conception of God! God is no monopoly of any nation; nor is God an extension of a particular people. No nation, however pious, can domesticate God. No people, however religious, can make an exclusive claim on God. God remembers Israel of course, but also remembers the Babylonians. God has a strong memory of the Christian church of course, but the welfare of the people of other faiths and cultures has never ceased to be present in God's memory either.

LIMITATIONS OF DEUTERONOMIC THEOLOGY OF HISTORY

What is Second Isaiah getting at here? What is the main thrust of his message? He seems to be saying that the history of Israel cannot be explained on the basis of its self-understanding. He is implying that the "orthodox" Deuteronomic interpretation of history has reached an impasse. Second Isaiah has stood up to challenge the official theology of the Deuteronomist school.

As we know, the Deuteronomic views on God, Israel, and history formed the spiritual foundation of Israel. What is taught and expounded by the theologians of the Deuteronomist traditions is considered the sum total of the faith that guides and directs the people. At the center of the teaching is the covenant that defines the relation between God and Israel. The "credo" in Deuteronomy 6:4–9 is an impressive expression of that covenant faith:

> Hear, O Israel, the Lord is our God, one Lord, and you must love the Lord your God with all your heart and soul and strength. These commandments which I give you this day are to be kept in your heart; you shall repeat them to your sons, and speak of them indoors and outdoors, when you lie down and when you rise. Bind them as a sign on the hand and wear them as a phylactery on the forehead; write them up on the door-posts of your houses and on your gates.

As has been said, this covenant faith, besides being central to the religious life of Israel, became fundamental to its political existence as a nation.

In the historical books of Joshua, Judges, 1 and 2 Samuel, and 1 and 2 Kings, we see the Deuteronomist's hand busily at work to give a theological ground to Israel's continuing political and military efforts in the land of Canaan. Confronted with the indigenous tribes and nations that resisted invasion and conquest by Israelite tribes, Deuteronomic theologians turned the universal covenant of God with creation into a particularistic covenant—a covenant that binds Israel to God in exclusion of other nations and peoples. In Joshua we see most clearly the development of Deuteronomic theology of history into an exclusive thinking conditioned chiefly by Israel's hostile relations with the peoples of Canaan.

This same Deuteronomic theology of history was also the framework for the narratives in the Book of Judges. The enormous odds that confronted the tribes of Israel in this period were interpreted "in terms of the Deuteronomic principle that apostasy leads to disaster and repentance brings deliverance."[7] This Deuteronomic principle is systematically employed not only to maintain the purity of faith in Yahweh but to perpetuate the hostile relations with the nations in Canaan.

From the standpoint of the religion of Israel, the Deuteronomists' way had to be accepted to ward off the promiscuous religions of Canaan. Yahweh against Baal! But when the religious fervor for Yahweh their God developed into a political fervor against the indigenous tribes and neighboring states, bloody confrontations became unavoidable. This kind of theology was dangerous. It was even dangerous to the classical prophets of the eighth and seventh centuries. They began to see these nations in the wider arena of history as more than just enemies of God to be exterminated. They had a premonition that Israel itself could not escape the fate of collapse when its course ran out.

This "cycle of sin-punishment-repentance-deliverance"[8] that was at the root of the Deuteronomic theology of history was also evident in the books of Samuel and Kings. Absolute faithfulness to God and the law was the chief criterion by which the moral conduct of the nation was evaluated and the performance of those in power in internal and external socio-political affairs was judged. The conviction that God was uniquely the God of Israel became the measure of all things, including the place and destiny of other nations in relation to Israel. Although this kind of massive theological concentration on the unique covenantal relationship between God and Israel gave to the loosely aligned tribes a very much needed internal coherence, it was certainly not adequate as the basis of understanding God's activity in wider circles.

The vision of God as the creator of all things had to be brought back into the faith that had become rigidly bound with the welfare of a particular nation. It was thus by no accident that the theme of creation later came to play an important role in the theology of the exilic period. Evidence of this is the Priestly version of the story of creation in Genesis 1:1–2:4a. That creation story is one of the outstanding products of transpositional theology during the time of the exile.

THE HUMBLE THEOLOGY OF THE SUFFERING SERVANT

The exile is in a true sense a debacle of the Deuteronomic theology of history with its centrism of Israel. It is for Israel a painful socio-political dislocation and a religious and theological confusion. A radical theological reorientation is needed for those in exile to rise above their confusion. Deuteronomic theology must be replaced by a new theological outlook, enabling them to see Israel and the nations in a different light. A transposition from the Israel-centered view of history to the view that regards other nations as constructive parts of God's design of history is required for a more realistic perception of God's work in the world. Such new theology of history contains a tacit admission that Israel alone cannot explain world history.

Religious centrism of Israel extended to the realm of history made Israel incapable of seeing the positive place as well as the negative meaning of the nations in God's creation and redemption. All this has to change, and it is Second Isaiah who has taken a bold leap from the centrism of Israel to a much broader outlook on the nations.

Second Isaiah has achieved this leap of faith in a very unconventional way. He has not begun with a suggestion for a reform of monarchy. He has not sought to restore messianism in religious and political terms. What he has done is to go to the root of human existence—suffering. And as he stares at the depth of suffering, the image of the Suffering Servant emerges to take hold of his faith and his theology.[9] He has made a transposition from the lofty Deuteronomic doctrine of God to the humble theology of a suffering God. Theology of glory has yielded to theology of suffering. Theology of a militant God is replaced by a theology of a compassionate God. The faith that always seeks to assert itself and dominate others gives way to a faith that renounces itself in order that others may be fulfilled. In the faith and theology of Second Isaiah we see some reflection of the oriental sense of fulfillment through renunciation.

Whoever the Suffering Servant may have been, he is no longer a national figure confined to the borders of Israel. His mission has far-reaching implications for the nations. He "will make justice shine on the nations" (Is. 42:1), and will "plant justice on earth" (42:4). God "will make him a light to the nations, and to be God's salvation to earth's farthest bounds" (49:6). And at his death, he "was assigned a grave with the wicked, and a burial-place among the refuse of mankind" (53:9). In this tragic end of the Servant, God's love and compassion comes to its full expression. The God of the Servant is the God of all those who suffer, the God of those regarded as the refuse of humankind.

The theology of Second Isaiah leads us to new frontiers of theology. It confronts us with the nations and with all human beings, even with those at the lowest echelons of society. It challenges us with the notion of a God who cannot be defined by our religious and social common sense. It shows us that God does not behave according to our theological principles. And it is this God that we catch a glimpse of in the Servant. As James Muilenberg, an American Old Testament theologian, puts it:

> . . . the servant is a figure of the coming age. . . . The decisive point of
> time is historical and yet more than historical. The history of Israel is

not enough to explain him, though the whole sacred history is somehow involved in the portrait as are the tumultuous events of the prophet's age.[10]

In the person of the Servant, world history begins to bear a meaning quite different from that advocated by Deuteronomic theology.

Indeed the Servant cannot be explained by Israel alone. He proves to be bigger than Israel. He breaks out of the tight compartment of faith and life that has given Israel its national and religious identity. He forces the Jews in the diaspora to find God in other nations. He urges them to give up their moral superiority, for he himself is going to be in the company of the wicked and the refuse of humankind in death. No nation is excluded from God's saving love; no one, not even the wicked, is left outside God's compassionate love.

This is a difficult theology to embrace. For what would happen to our distinctiveness as the special people of God? How could we exchange our familiar God for such a strange God? And how long would it take for us to get this strange God to stand on our side? But the Servant is not going to be deterred by such questions. He sees this God beckoning him from all places. He hears this God calling him from the nations. And he knows that where that God is, something extraordinary is bound to happen. He must make every effort to prepare himself and his fellow Jews for big surprises. They are standing at the threshold of a new era.

THE ONE FROM THE EAST

The prelude to this new era is the summons issued to the nations to reason out the ultimate power behind the rise and fall of empires. The surprising thing is that the summons carries no imperialistic overtone. God and the nations, says the prophet Second Isaiah, "will meet at the place of judgment, I and they" (41:1). God is humble enough to receive the nations at the court of judgment. God, instead of imposing a verdict on them, invites them to express their own views. The nations are not just accidental factors in history that can be dispensed with at will. They are as much a part of history as Israel is. That is why they are summoned to come and decide with God who it is that moves history.

In the presence of the nations God poses a question:

> Who raised up that one from the east,
> one greeted by victory wherever he goes?
> Who is it that puts nations into his power
> and makes kings go down before him? [41:2]

Who is this one from the east? No answer is given in this passage, but the nations at God's court must surely know who that one from the east is. They have seen him rise to power and ride to victory. They have perhaps come under his intimidating military power. Who else could he be? He is no other than that great Cyrus who "had succeeded to the great empire of Astyages the Mede, had thrust his battalions far into the north and west, and had defeated the Lydians at Sardes."[11] Cyrus has made himself into an invincible conqueror.

Even the prophet, though a Jew, does not conceal his astonishment as he describes Cyrus's brilliant military exploits across the ancient Near East:

> He scatters them [the nations] with his sword like dust
> and with his bow like chaff before the wind;
> he puts them to flight and passes on unscathed,
> swifter than any traveller on foot [41:2].

Is this a mere expression of the satisfaction of seeing Israel's captors put to rout by this mighty ruler who has risen on the horizon of history? Perhaps it is more than that. There seems here a genuine amazement about the turn that the political fortunes of the nations have taken. Israel once held the political power that made it a dominant voice in the shaping of the life of the nations. Then came the Assyrians and the Babylonians. To them Israel and Judah lost their territorial and national sovereignty. And now it is the turn of this Cyrus from the east. He has risen to assume the political and military leadership over the whole region.

The prophet cannot suppress his amazement at the rise of this new power; he comes back to it more than once. In Isaiah 45:1–5 he once again describes Cyrus's military successes in vivid language. But now he goes much farther and calls him "God's anointed" (45:1), saying that "Israel's God calls him by name" (45:3,4). And in Isaiah 44:28 the prophet does not hesitate to name Cyrus "God's shepherd."

Not only the socio-political situations but theological climate too have taken a very different turn. Such a "liberal" view of history could not have been possible for the Deuteronomic theology of history. In the words of Claus Westermann, a German Old Testament exegete, "Deutero-Isaiah makes an assertion which his hearers found both incredible and highly obnoxious, namely that in the rise of the king of Persia, which had never before come within the sphere of Yahweh's action, he saw the hand of the God of Israel."[12]

To Deuteronomic theologians and to the "fundamentalist" Jews in exile, the prophet must have appeared an archheretic. A faith that serves a national ideology, identifies itself completely with the national cause, and becomes captive to certain liturgical and creedal formulations is not capable of a leap of faith such as taken by the prophet Second Isaiah. The distance from the God of the patriarchs to the God of the nations is too great to cover. The gulf between King David as God's anointed and King Cyrus as God's shepherd is too wide to cross. And the religious culture of the Jewish people and that of a pagan nation are too different to become interrelated. This is the "right" theology. In the eyes of "orthodox" believers and "right" theologians, the prophet has committed a terrible blunder of faith.

But what is "orthodox" in faith and what is "right" in theology? There is no orthodoxy apart from the orthodoxy of God. There is no rightness aside from the rightness of God. It is not what we believers and theologians believe and do that makes God appear orthodox and right. It is what God is and does that makes what we believe orthodox and what we do right. If God calls Cyrus the pagan king God's anointed, that is orthodoxy. If God appoints him to be God's shepherd, that is right theology.

God comes at the beginning of our faith and theology, not at the end. This after all must be what theology is all about. "In the beginning God created heaven and earth" (Gen. 1:1)—our faith begins here and not elsewhere. "In the beginning was the word" (Jn. 1:1)—our theology starts here and not elsewhere. This God at the beginning frees us from our own religious interests and pretensions.

If this God is at the beginning of our faith, we can believe in some extraordinary things, even the appointment of a pagan king to be God's servant. If this God is at the forefront of our theology, we can think of some unthinkable things, even God's personal presence among the pagan people of Babylon or Persia. When God is at the head of our faith and theology, a leap of faith from Israel to the nations becomes not only possible but necessary. The prophet Second Isaiah made such a leap of faith. That leap made his theology of history a new step beyond the traditional framework of faith and theology.

GOD REVEALS THE END FROM THE BEGINNING

Fresh ideas continue to pour out of the prophet's sensitive mind. Our attention is now drawn to Isaiah 46:9–13. Cyrus, the king of Persia, is still the central focus here. He is referred to as "a bird of prey" or an "eagle" (46:11), undoubtedly because of his powerfulness and ruthlessness. But the prophet advises his hearers not just to be dazzled by Cyrus's great achievements. Cyrus is the occasion for them to "remember all that happened long ago" (46:9). They must realize that "God reveals the end from the beginning, from ancient times God reveals what is to be" (46:10).

History is not a haphazard thing. It has an end and a beginning, but to understand the end we must go back to the beginning. The root of history is its beginning. Cyrus is not to be considered as just a transitory phenomenon. He has his root in the beginning of time. He is rooted in God.

The words "remember the former things of old," says Westermann, "remind Israel of her history."[13] The exodus must surely be prominent in this. The wandering in the wilderness must be part and parcel of it. And presumably the long and arduous struggle to find settlement in the land of promise, followed by the glory and shame of dynastic history, should still be a fresh memory. This in short is the memory of how God dealt with Israel both in love and judgment. Faith in this God is the core of the act of remembering. It is not a sentimental remembering that the prophet asks them to do. They are at the important juncture of history in the life of captivity. This is certainly no time for cheap sentiment. Mere sentiment is no match for the hard reality of life and history. Reliance on sentiment in face of test and change makes one a loser.

Even patriotic sentiment does not help. There must have been no lack of the outpouring of patriotic sentiment among the exiled Jews. "How could we sing the Lord's song in a foreign land?" (Ps. 137:4) This is an expression of a noble sentiment. Our hearts go out to those who sing it. We are prompted to answer the lament and chagrin with a strong *no*. No, you could not sing the Lord's song in a foreign land! You should recall your own glorious past and rekindle the flame of patriotism!

But faced with the strange phenomenon of Cyrus, the Jews in exile have a more urgent thing to do. They must consult their past history and find out how foreign kings such as Cyrus have come into being. True, in the exodus God raised Moses among their own race to carry out the mission of deliverance from Egypt. It was Joshua from the tribe of Ephraim who was commissioned to lead Israel into Canaan after the death of Moses. In the times of Judges, those who responded to the crises and came to the rescue were from their own kinsfolk. This is the saving "pattern" with which they are familiar. They must have assumed that the same pattern would also be working in the future.

But the prophet proved them wrong. God is not bound to any pattern firmly entrenched in their religious and national consciousness. In fact God often breaks out of that pattern and leads life to a different plateau, gives people a new vision, and sets history on a new course.

This must have sounded very novel in the ears of the prophet's hearers. This is because they are used to understanding God's work from this end of their history and not from the beginning that God made with the creation. The prophet points out to them that they begin at the wrong end. With God it is just the reverse. God "reveals the end from the beginning and from ancient times reveals what is to be." They must return to that beginning point of creation and realize once again how all nations and peoples converge in one great creating and redeeming act of God. As they do this, their blindness to God's activity in the whole of history will be lifted. Cyrus will no longer be an illegitimate element in world history, not even in their own history.

There are countless pieces and fragments to history. Cyrus is such a piece. Israel is such a fragment. They are all held together by the hand of the creator at the beginning. It is to that beginning point that they should return to come to grips with their interrelatedness. The end must be illuminated by the beginning. This is the basic principle of Second Isaiah's theology of history. It must be the principle of our theology of history too.

GOD SETS UP NO ALIBI

Return to the beginning enables the prophet to extend the horizon of faith farther. It is to the creation that his vision is now directed. In Second Isaiah's theology of history, creation plays an important role. To understand the meaning of King Cyrus in relation to Israel and world history, this maximum extension of the horizon of faith is necessary. Creation is the key to the meaning and place of the nations in history. It gives birth to history. God's own affirmation of creation must therefore precede our historical thinking.

Second Isaiah hears God saying:

> With my own hands I founded the earth,
> with my right hand I formed the expanse of sky;
>   when I summoned them,
>   they sprang at once into being [48:13].

Cyrus is a long way from the creation. To most Jews he bears no relation to God the creator. But Second Isaiah has a different insight. He traces the origin of Cyrus all the way back to the beginning of time.

Creation is where everything got started. It is God who brought all nations and peoples—all things—into existence. All that is created is therefore the genealogy of God.[14] This is fundamental to the biblical faith. If Israel claims to have a part in this genealogy of God, then Assyria, Babylon, and Persia too must be part of it. This is perfectly logical. It becomes illogical when a particular nation makes an exclusive claim to it, refusing to let others have any place in it. By placing Cyrus in God's genealogy of creation, Second Isaiah has done nothing strange or wrong. On the contrary, he shares with his fellow Jews a deep insight into the nature of faith that sees all nations and peoples as essentially related to God's creative power.

Cyrus is therefore not a step-child of God; for that matter, no one is. Between God and human beings no "step-relationship" exists. God is God, not a step-God. A step-God is a God of prejudice. Such a God makes a clear distinction between legitimate children and step-children. There is no bond of natural love between a step-God and the step-children. If such a God has love to spare for them, that love becomes a favor. It is not given freely. It is love with strings attached. It is thus a strained kind of love. That love is not an outpouring of all that God is. It is "step-love." And a theology that regards other nations as a hundred steps, or even two steps or one step, removed from God is a step-theology. Christian theology has a tendency to become such a step-theology. This is what the theology of the love of God must not become. One of the urgent tasks of Third World theologians consists in removing the steps that traditional theology has set up between God and nations.

Second Isaiah sets out precisely to undo what we have called step-theology. He is emphatic that God takes personal responsibility for the rise of Cyrus.

He tells his hearers what he has perceived to be God's words:

> I, I myself, have spoken,
> I have called him [Cyrus],
> I have made him appear,
> and wherever he goes he shall prosper [48:15].

The coming into being of Cyrus comes from God's own word—the word that brought all things into existence, the word spoken to the prophets in judgment and in salvation, the word that becomes history of Israel and history of the nations. Eventually it is this same word of God that is to become flesh in Jesus Christ. God works in the world through word. The relation of Cyrus to God is therefore a *theo*-logical one. He proceeds from God's word and is given a definite place and role in the providence of God.

Second Isaiah's audience must have been taken aback by such a bold theological statement. With all their respect for him, they must have found it difficult to take in all that he has to say. As if to forestall their doubt and protest, the prophet goes on to say on God's behalf:

> Draw near to me and hear this:
> from the beginning I have never spoken in secret;
> from the moment of its first happening I was there [48:16].

God does not set up an alibi to deny involvement in what has taken place. God was there when the whole creation came into being. God saw it happen. In fact God gave birth to it. Even if the creation becomes corrupted, God does not disavow responsibility for it. From the beginning to the end, God is fully and entirely present. God does not need an alibi to get out of the difficulty of dealing with the power of evil and corruption in creation. We have no alibi God. And this non-alibi God is the suffering God. God suffers in the suffering of the Suffering Servant, in the suffering of the suffering Son Jesus Christ, and in the suffering of a suffering people.

As important as the rejection of alibi is the rejection of secrecy in God's dealings with the world. Second Isaiah stresses that God has never spoken anything in secret. God does not whisper behind the back of creation. Nor does God prevaricate in front of the people. There is nothing that God has thought in the depth of the divine Spirit that cannot be spoken out loud in the human spirit. There is nothing that God has said in private that cannot be repeated in public. There is nothing God has done that cannot be displayed in the full view of the people. God does not whisper into someone's ear so that others cannot hear what is being said.

In the Word become flesh, God becomes a visible Word. Jesus Christ is that Word. He is also God's audible Word. In Jesus Christ God speaks and acts openly and publicly. In him God turns to our history, comes dangerously close to it, and makes it God's own history. In the Word become flesh, God turns to us completely, hiding nothing from us. God becomes so helplessly open and so dangerously exposed to opponents and assailants. As Jesus hangs on the cross before the eyes of the whole world, there can be no false expectation from God anymore.

This is the God whom Second Isaiah foresaw a few centuries before Jesus Christ. Even then the prophet realized that God had not made plans behind the back of the world. The mission was not a secret mission. It was open to those who were willing to see. It was intelligible to those who could rise above their national and religious interests.

God appears secretive only to those who want to monopolize and to possess God. They feel cheated when God shows favor to other nations and sides with their rivals. They get impatient with God when God is patient with those who have no place in their belief systems and theological constructs. Second Isaiah wanted to help them put away their misgivings about the God who had raised Cyrus to political prominence. The God of Cyrus is the God of creation.

This faith is as orthodox as the faith in the God of Abraham, Isaac, and Jacob. The leap from the God of Abraham to the God of Cyrus is a big leap. But that leap has to be taken in order to understand better God's work in human history. In the rise of Cyrus, the king of Persia, Second Isaiah finds a compelling reason to make that leap.

GOD IS THE FIRST AND THE LAST

History has a meaning that cannot be exhausted by Israel. Second Isaiah has driven this home to his compatriots in exile. His faith is expansive. It expands to the creation, to the beginning of time.

It is this expansive faith that gives an inner coherence to the passages we have been discussing—Isaiah 41:1-5, 46:9-13, and 48:12-16. As the prophet continues to meditate on God and human history, his expansive mood seems to have no end. He is eager to share it with his hearers whose faith tends to shrink instead of expanding. He wants them to be able to believe in the God who is greater than their hopes or the miscarriage of their hopes. He tries to inspire them with a vision that is not conditioned by their dreams, nor by the disappearance of their dreams. This is no time for a shrinking and brooding faith. Such faith only makes them petty prisoners hardened by remorse and self-pity.

Faith that expands in spite of human tragedy and adversity comes from the God who expands from the first to the last. In the perceptive mind of the prophet, God is saying clearly: "I am the first, I am the last also" (48:12b; 41:4b). How much more expansive could God be? Even God has a limit. But that limit is in fact God's limitlessness—in space and also in time.

The first and the last embrace the whole span of time. It is the whole of eternity. God as the first and the last is the God of time and eternity. Time belongs to God. It has no separate existence apart from God. It exists in God.

Time is time because it is God's. And it is our time because it is first God's time. My time, your time, his time, her time—all our times—are God's time. The time of unbelievers as well as the time of believers is the time of God. Both the time of pagans and the time of Christians is God's time. There is only one time, and that is God's time. Time is eternity, and eternity time.

Because history takes place in time, what is said above about time can be applied to history also. The first and the last encompasses the whole of history, the history from the beginning to the end, the history which consists of all nations, including Israel. All history is God's history. The history of Persia is just as much God's history as is the history of Israel. The history of the "pagan" East is no less God's than the history of the "Christian" West. No history, not even the history of China or Vietnam, can exist outside God.

History exists in God. It comes from God and returns to God. God does not stand *over against* history but is *in* history. And this God works in history through prophets and sages, through kings and peasants, through us all.

God as the first and the last is, furthermore, "the ultimate source and ground of existence."[15] What is ultimate is final. It is final not because it comes at the end of a series of things and events; the ultimate is final in the sense that it embraces all, that there is nothing else as embracing as it is. The ultimate is that reality beyond which nothing exists. It negates "nothingness." Nothingness is meaningless to it. The ultimate is all; it is everything. If we have it, we have all; if we lose it, we lose all. God is such an ultimate. God is ultimate, final, embracing. God is our all. We cannot come to this God halfheartedly. On such a God we must stake our all.

Arjuna, the hero of the great epic poem of the *Bhagavad Gita*,[16] seems to have had a vision of the ultimate. His soul is deeply troubled on the eve of battle against his own kin. And in the depth of his agony, he catches a glimpse of the ultimate. He bursts out in praise of Lord Krishna:

And why should they not do Thee homage, O Exalted One, who art greater than Brahma, the original creator? O Infinite Being, Lord of the gods, Refuge of the universe, Thou art the Imperishable, the being and the non-being and what is beyond that.[17]

Before the ultimate, human language falters. The ultimate is both being and nonbeing. It is both here and beyond. It is both in and out. It is all and in all.

Artists, poets, and persons of deep devotion often give us a glimpse of this ultimate God. They call upon the created universe to join in the praise of God:

Praise the Lord out of heaven!
praise him in the heights. . . .
Praise him, sun and moon;
praise him, all you shining stars;
praise him, heaven of heavens,
and you waters above the heavens [Ps. 148:1–4].

58

DISRUPTION—DISPERSION

Why do these elements in the universe have to praise God? Why do they owe homage to God? This is the psalmist's answer:

> Let them all praise the name of the Lord,
>   for he spoke the word and they were created;
>   he established them for ever and ever
> by an ordinance which shall never pass away [Ps. 148:5–6].

This takes us at once back to the creation story in Genesis 1. The sun, the stars, and all that exists between heaven and earth come from God. God is in them because God's word causes them to be and gives them life. To poets, painters, and believers, the beauty of nature is the beauty of God; the glory of nature is the glory of God.

But nature is not all beauty and glory. It can become moody and angry too. Volcanos erupt, storms break out, earthquakes shake the foundations of the earth. This is nature in fury. It is perhaps more than that. It is perhaps God in fury.

This is how the Hebrew slaves saw the plight of their cruel masters in Egypt. When these arrogant slave masters refused to let them go, they perceived in their faith that God was angry. Then "the Lord sent thunder and hail, with fire flashing down to the ground. The Lord rained down hail on the land of Egypt, hail and fiery flashes through the hail, so heavy that there had been nothing like it in all Egypt from the time that Egypt became a nation" (Ex. 9:23–25).

That God has everything to do with nature is one of the most universal beliefs. Common men and women toiling under the burning sun and struggling in the torrential rain know by instinct that in nature they have God to reckon with.

In *Shuihu chuan* (All Men Are Brothers), a famous Chinese novel from the twelfth century with narrations of the fugitives and bandits constantly at war with corrupt government officials, an army officer was commissioned by the regent of the northern capital to lead a birthday-gift convoy. In order to avoid the ambush of bandits, he drove hard the porters bearing heavy gifts of gold, pearls, silk, and gems under the intense heat from the midday sun. His men were exasperated and exhausted. And this is how they saw the merciless sun:

> From the deep south,
>   the God of Conflagration comes
>   riding on his fiery dragon,
> Waving his flaming banner,
>   which sets high heaven ablaze.
> With the glowing wheel of the sun
>   transfixed to the noonday sky,

> The nations of the world are baked
> in a red hot oven.
> No clouds girt the Sacred Mountains,
> their vegetation quite withered.
> The Lord of the Seas now talks about
> extinction by evaporation.
> When will fresh autumnal gusts
> start blowing of an evening
> And sweep away the oppressive heat
> that plagues our good earth?[18]

Is this a pure literary imagination? Perhaps not. Nature is the arena of God's activity in glory and also in fury.

If this is true with nature, it should be much more true with history, for history should be much more alive with God than is nature. In history we no longer deal with the sun, the moon, and the stars. In history we deal with peoples and nations, not just peoples and nations in general, but with particular nations and particular peoples. There is the history of Israel, and the history of Persia. There is the history of Japan, and the history of Germany.

History is not an abstract concept. History is a flesh-and-blood people. For this reason we must speak of the history of the Jewish people, the history of the Egyptian people. We do not just study the history of Britain and the United States or the history of Vietnam; what we study is the history of the Anglo-Saxon people, the history of the Vietnamese people. It is *persons* who give a content to history. They fill history with endless tales of joys and woes. They make history cry out from their hearts. And it is in history that we meet God who comes to share our anguish and hopes. In our own historical specificity we encounter the God of the first and the last.

NATIONS BETWEEN ISRAEL AND WORLD HISTORY

Christian theology has not taken seriously or had much respect for the historical specificity of the nations other than Israel and the western nations deeply influenced by Christianity. We have already had something critical to say about the concept of *Heilsgeschichte*. It has been the tendency of Christian theologians to jump from *Heilsgeschichte* to world history or universal history. And if the concept of *Heilsgeschichte* is narrowly and precisely defined to mean Israel and the Christian church, the notion of world history or universal history is, in contrast, vague and imprecise. It is *either* implicitly understood as a projection of the history of Israel and the history of the Christian church *or* it is considered as history in general without specific references. In either case, the nations outside the Judeo-Christian traditions slip through the fingers of Christian theologians, leaving no traces in their doctrines on God, Jesus Christ, the church, or even their theology of history.

This is quite in contrast with ancient theologians such as Second Isaiah who did not hesitate to bring a pagan king such as Cyrus into God's design of salvation in history. Theology *then* was unstructured, for it left all structuring to God. But theology *now* has become so structured that it leaves little room for the adventurous God.

The theology of Wolfhart Pannenberg, a German advocate of the new hermeneutical school, seems an example of such a highly structured system of the Christian faith, although universal history is one of its main concerns. He is, to begin with, very critical of the concept of *Heilsgeschichte*, calling it "a ghetto of redemptive history."[19] He also refers by implication to Cullmann's linear concept of salvation in history with Christ at its center as "that notorious mathematical point which is without extension on the intersected plane."

Over against such a narrow understanding of God's saving activity in history, Pannenberg argues in favor of "the principle of universal correlation" which "carries with it the acceptance of casual relations between historical phenomena." The adjective "casual" here is important, for he stresses the contingent character of history open to change, to new happenings and the future. For him God does not work within history schematically in accordance with a predetermined plan. This emphasis on the dynamic nature of God in history should be appreciated.

It appears as if Pannenberg has definitely left "the *Heilsgeschichte* school" and ventured into something different. He gives us the impression that when he speaks of history he really means business, for history for him is not limited to the history of Israel and Christianity; it is the history which stretches far back into the creation. This is what he tells us at one point:

History is the most comprehensive horizon of Christian theology. All theological questions and answers are meaningful only within the framework of the history which God has with humanity and through humanity with his whole creation—the history moving toward a future still hidden from the world but already revealed in Jesus Christ.[20]

In his theology, history in its totality is given a place of honor and treated with respect. He further says elsewhere:

. . . the totality of history to which theological talk about God and his revelation in Jesus are related now constitutes an unavoidable theme of historical hermeneutic, for the reason that all historical study remains oriented to the problem of universal history.[21]

At last God seems to have been liberated from "the ghetto of redemptive history" and from "the notorious mathematical point" that confines God to a certain plane of history.

Such an impression is, however, a little premature. The crux of the matter lies in the concepts of "the totality of history" and "universal history." What does Pannenberg mean by these big concepts? What do they point to? What are their concrete connotations? Unfortunately, these notions of his sound more like philosophical abstractions than concrete historical experiences that constitute the history of each and all nations. If universal history is an abstract concept—a totality that has no reference to particular nations—how can one envision God acting in it? How is it to be related to God? What happens then to the God who, according to Pannenberg, works "contingently" in history, constantly bringing into existence new things and new happenings? Where on earth are these new things and new happenings to be located?

As a matter of fact, concepts such as universal history or the totality of history can be dangerous if they are not used carefully. What often happens in Christian theology is that the totality of history tends to be a projection of Judeo-Christian history; it tends to be this particular history magnified on the universal plane.

We should remind ourselves that the Hegelian philosophers in the nineteenth century made a universal claim for their understanding of history derived from their historical and cultural experiences. The criticism that Pannenberg's concept of the totality of history smacks of Hegelianism is not entirely off the mark. Indeed, it is from Hegel that "Pannenberg derives his key term, universal history."[22] This being the case, theologians in the Third World must not hastily jump to the conclusion that in Pannenberg they have found a theological ally. It is, in fact, not unreasonable to suspect that Third World nations would find no place, or at most a secondary place, in such a theological scheme of universal history.

That Pannenberg's notion of universal history "overcomes the cleavage between salvation history and world history"[23] cannot be accepted without question. In spite of his opposition to Cullmann's "mathematical point of redemptive history," Pannenberg stresses that the meaning of the totality of history is "already revealed in Jesus Christ." This sounds on the surface a perfectly correct theological statement. Christ is the meaning of all that exists in history. But when we realize that a theological assertion such as this is made largely on the Judeo-Christian, *western* experience of history, we are no longer sure of its universal validity.

This is a clear case of *pars pro toto,* a theological position that becomes increasingly difficult for persons in the Third World to accept when they struggle to find their place in world history. One of the pressing tasks of Third World Christians and theologians is to test and appropriate "the revelation of the meaning of history in Jesus Christ" on the basis of their Judeo-Christian-*Third World* historical experiences. This means that "the revelation of the meaning of history in Jesus Christ" is not closed, finished, or terminated. God can and does work in ways that will take us by surprise. In fact this is the whole point of revelation. Revelation and surprise—these two go together. This makes the business of faith so agonizing and so exciting. It also makes the task of theology an open and unending task.

The "cleavage between *Heilsgeschichte* and world history" has in fact not been overcome in Pannenberg's theology of universal history. After a long detour of universal history he comes back to where he started: *Heilsgeschichte*. This is the depot from which all theological buses in traditional models start out into various routes and to which they dutifully return. Cullmann must be laughing up his sleeve when he remarks: "To be sure [Pannenberg] does not play up the term *'Heilsgeschichte,'* but in spite of all deviation in detail [his] position comes near to that advocated by myself in *Christ and Time*."[24]

Our conclusion is that Pannenberg's "principle of universal correlation" is not so attractive as it promises to be. In this day and age, a Christian theology of history cannot make one giant leap from the Judeo-Christian, western history to universal history, leaving aside completely the history of the Eskimos, the Australian bushfolk, the Polynesians in the southern Pacific, or the Chinese-Mongolians in that vast continent of Asia. In traditional theology such a jump is encouraged; it is taken for granted. Deviation into other histories is a "missiological" mandate, not a "theological" necessity.

For this reason, missiology and theology have so far remained in practice strange bedfellows. In a respectable theological seminary, the department of missiology suffers an inferiority complex under the shadow of the imposing department of dogmatic theology. In relation to the nations and peoples outside Judeo-Christian traditions, Christian theology has inevitably been poor in spite of its richness, timid despite its illustrious scholarship, and shortsighted although it can boast of two thousand years of history.

GOD LOVES CYRUS

The surprises Second Isaiah has in store for his people seem without end. He must have been aware that what he has been saying could be too taxing for their religious sensitivity. But he feels constrained to go on and let the truth out as he has perceived it. He once again gets them together and asks them to listen to his discourse:

> Yahweh loves him [Cyrus],
> he performs his purpose on Babylon
> and on the [seed] of the Chaldeans [Is. 48:14b].[25]

The word "love" is a very sensitive word. It is a very special word. Parents love their children and children love their parents. Brothers and sisters love one another. Close friends are bound with a bond of love. And above all, God loves the people. Love binds God to them. As such a special word, love is not to be used at random. It presupposes a close and intimate relationship.

Second Isaiah could have avoided such a sensitive word. He could have said, for instance, that God liked Cyrus, fancied him, or cared for him. Anything would do except that sensitive and therefore strong word "love." But Second Isaiah must have decided that, in an extraordinary time such as this, being diplomatic may not be the best policy. He goes ahead and says that Yahweh loves Cyrus, knowing that this may sound offensive to his hearers. But they must accept the fact that in addition to being God's anointed one and shepherd, Cyrus is God's loved one.

The importance of Second Isaiah's reference to Cyrus as God's loved one cannot be overstressed. With this the prophet has broken another mental and spiritual obstacle that isolates Israel from the nations. The assumption of Jewish faith is that "pagan" nations are strangers in the household of God. They are not the object of love but tolerance. They are allowed to be there not on principle but as a compromise. For some reason or other they have strayed into the company of God's people, but are not expected to gain the right of permanent residence there.

This is a kind of discrimination theology. It is true to say that religion has a strong tendency to give rise to discrimination. Discrimination seems deeply rooted in the religious subconsciousness of believers. And it often develops into racial or socio-political discrimination. The desire to protect one's own interest, the need to defend oneself against foreign intrusion, and the passion to own things, even to own God, are too strong to resist. In the practice of faith in particular, the temptation to discriminate has never been an easy temptation to cope with.

In many ways we as Christians are not above the temptation to discriminate. Even without meaning to do so, we discriminate through the sheer force of convention of language and habit of thought and behavior.

Take, for example, the words "Christian" and "non-Christian." These two words have been in our vocabulary for a long time, and they are very convenient expressions. There are Christians in "non-Christian" lands, among "non-Christians." In many matters related to moral or ethical concerns, there is a distinctively "Christian" way of thinking over against a "non-Christian" way of thinking. There is also a kind of behavior that is Christian in contrast to non-Christian behavior. The professions too can be viewed in a similar way. One speaks of "Christian" lawyers and "non-Christian" lawyers, "Christian" doctors and "non-Christian" doctors, although when it comes to "Christian" mathematicians and "non-Christian" mathematicians the distinction becomes a bit silly.

The point to remember is that words such as "Christian" and "non-Christian" used together are not free from value judgment. And in the way we often use them, a great deal of emotion is attached to them. They are therefore not value-free words. What is more, they are emotive words, and as such, they often become discriminatory words. T. K. Thomas, editor of CCA (Christian Conference of Asia) News observes that "non-Christian" is "an expression that divides and a judgment that is premature." He further points out:

More primarily, it is a discourteous expression. We are what we are, not what we-are-not. We are not non-apes, but human beings. Our Buddhist and Hindu friends are Buddhist and Hindus, not non-Christians. They do not find their identity in relation to Christians; they find it within their heritage and because of their faith, on their own.[26]

Besides being judgmental, discourteous, and divisive, this long established use of the word "non-Christian" in our Christian vocabulary makes us Christians the center of all people and all things. It is an expression of Christian centrism.

Christians still need to get used to the idea that God is related to the world's peoples at many centers. There is no one center that makes others unnecessary. One center may become more prominent than others at certain times, and from that prominent position we may gain a better view of other centers. But this in no way means that there are no other centers. What does certainly happen is that, as in the case of Cyrus, other centers may have some reverse impact on that one center with the result that a radical change in faith is called for.

Second Isaiah seems to sum up his theological orientation in a simple sentence: Yahweh loves Cyrus. Cyrus is not just an instrumental cause that will disappear as soon as he has performed his functions. The relation between God and Cyrus is a far more fundamental kind—it is a relationship of love. It is the intimate bond of love that ties Cyrus to God. It is no easy thing for the Jews in the diaspora to accept this fact into their faith and theology, but they must try.

In Cyrus God has shown them another center where people become closely related to God. There will be yet other centers. Their one-center theology must become a multi-center theology. Their one-way system of faith is faced with the possibility of a multi-way system of faith. Second Isaiah proves to be a daring pioneer of faith whose vision of God at work in history is enriched and enlarged by a pagan king whom he calls God's loved one.

CHAPTER THREE

Broadened Vision of History

History seems more complicated than most of us Christians care to admit. The power that holds movements of peoples together and causes the vicissitudes of nations is much stronger than we are able to realize. When we sense this power that moves history, creates its fabric and directs its course, we feel puzzled, mystified, and astounded. We are forced to acknowledge that our faith is challenged. The norms with which we judge and evaluate historical phenomena outside the realm of our faith undergo a serious test. The assumptions of our religious and ethical values are questioned.

We have seen this happen to the Jews taken to Babylon in captivity. We have tried to listen to the persuasive voice of Second Isaiah and to follow his farsighted vision.

For those of us in Asia who experience the impacts of religions and cultures unrelated to Christianity, the voice and vision of the prophet are fresh and challenging. To discern the purpose of God in history is for us as for him not a matter of academic interest but of practical challenge. It is with the same concern in mind that we will return to the Book of Daniel in this chapter.

CRISIS AND HUMAN RESPONSES

In our earlier discussion, we mentioned how the Book of Daniel was compiled to be addressed to the Jews faced with the crisis of persecution at the hands of Antiochus IV Epiphanes. We must now focus our attention on Nebuchadnezzar's dream and its interpretation in the second chapter of Daniel.

The origin of this most intriguing narrative can be traced to "the Diaspora under the Persian or early Greek empires."[1] This at once suggests to us that the narrative might have shared the concern we have seen so forcefully expressed by Second Isaiah: to give account of the reason why other nations also play an important role in history within God's providence.

Why then did the narrative find its way into the Book of Daniel? Why should it occupy the attention of an oppressed people under foreign domina-

65

tion? What they urgently need is a kind of moral strength that can sustain them. What they must immediately have is a kind of spiritual power that enables them to endure their tribulation. But the story of Nebuchadnezzar's dream and its interpretation, according to Berdyaev, "represents the first attempt in the history of mankind to attribute a design to history."[2] What we have in the story is a kind of theology of history that did not originate in a time of persecution but in the "remote" past, in the late exilic period.

Why do they need it? What purpose will it serve? How can they theorize about "a design to history" at a time like this? They are preoccupied with resistance to a tyrannical ruler. They struggle to survive a political power that has become almost insane. What they have to do is create a united front against the foreign oppressor.

This was the course of action taken by resistance movements such as that headed by the Maccabees. Later the Zealots represented a similar uncompromising attitude toward the Roman colonial rule. Even Jesus himself seemed to have some sympathy for them. Some of his disciples were even said to have belonged to the zealotic party.

At a time of crisis, therefore, what the people should have are straightforward directives that tell them what to do and how to act, and not a kind of theology of history couched in indirect language and a mystifying imagery.

Our puzzlement here leads us to explore a little the relation between crisis and human response to it. It seems that the crisis that besets a person or a nation evokes at least two kinds of response.

When it strikes, a crisis may completely overwhelm us and make us numb. It invades our whole being and consumes our whole humanity. We feel helpless and a sense of emptiness overtakes us. We are reduced to a kind of one-dimensional existence. We lose our perspective. We not only think one-dimensionally, but act one-dimensionally. Height, breadth, and depth have disappeared from our life. The immediacy of the crisis determines and dictates our response to life as a whole. The life threatened by a crisis becomes a very intense kind of life. The world seen through the crisis-ridden life tends to lose all its color. The crisis reduces life and history to a mathematical moment of the present. The present gets detached from the past and from the future. It makes the present moment bear all the meaning and meaninglessness of life and history. This is one kind of response to a crisis situation.

There is, however, another kind of response, one that enables us to go through a crisis strengthened and enriched. Confronted with a crisis, we are given the power to become free from imprisonment to the present. We are enabled to face life in all its height, breadth, and depth. We are urged to view history not just from the standpoint of the present but from the perspective of eternity. We may then realize that the crisis reveals to us what has been hidden from our sight. It deepens our sense of mystery and tells us that life and history are not exhausted in the present moment of fear and danger.

True, a crisis brings disruption into our life. But as has been shown in the first chapter, disruption liberates us from our one-dimensional, linear, or straight-line understanding of history. The tide of life and history rises and falls. Crisis is built into it. At every rise and fall of the tide, we are taken to a new shore and encounter something strange and different. But despite all its strangeness and difference, we may hear echoes that sound familiar. Why do they sound familiar? Perhaps because they are echoes from our God.

It seems that it is this second kind of response to crisis that underlies the story of Nebuchadnezzar's dream and its interpretation. An extraordinary time requires an extraordinary way to read the meaning of history. This story is one such extraordinary way. It is designed to help the Jews under persecution read an eschatological meaning out of their present history. It also has as its purpose to enable them to come to grips with the significance of God's kingdom within the framework of what they are going through. In their personal and national crisis, history and eschatology have converged.

History must now be interpreted eschatologically, and eschatology must be understood historically. That is why the interpretation of Nebuchadnezzar's dream, in which the four earthly kingdoms of the Babylonians, the Medes, the Persians, and the Greeks have gone through the stages of construction and destruction, concludes by saying: ". . . the God of heaven will establish a kingdom which will never be destroyed; that kingdom shall never pass to another people; it shall shatter and make an end of all these kingdoms, while it shall itself endure for ever" (Dan. 2:44).

The historico-eschatological link has been established here between the earthly kingdoms and God's kingdom. Even at the time of persecution under Antiochus Epiphanes, when the Jews were longing for the timely intervention of God, they had to be told that they could not bypass this historico-eschatological link. The kingdom of God does not consist in destroying the kingdoms of this world. As the Lord of history, God does not take a shortcut and make a quick job of ending earthly powers. God's kingdom must work in and through the kingdoms and empires that rise and fall, one after the other. The kingdom of God does not descend from heaven. It does not appear suddenly out of the blue.

Most of the Jews under the heavy hand of their oppressor are not likely to rise above their exigency and gain a *theo*-logical insight into the meaning of God's kingdom that can be discerned in the rise and fall of nations and empires. But for some at least such an insight is indispensable to make sense out of their turbulent present situation and to retain faith in God who, they believe, works in history. In the Book of Daniel is implanted a theology of history that strengthens faith in the God of history and extends the vision of God's kingdom to other nations.

NEBUCHADNEZZAR—GOD'S SERVANT

Nebuchadnezzar's dream was an extraordinary one. In his dream the king saw a fearful statue towering over him. The head of the statue was made of gold, the chest and arms of silver, the abdomen and thighs of bronze, the legs of iron, and the feet of fragile potsherds. As the king looked on in astonishment, a mysterious stone flew out of a mountain nearby and struck its most vulnerable part—the feet made of fragile potsherds. The statue collapsed, disintegrated, and disappeared, leaving not a trace. In its place the stone "grew into a great mountain filling the whole earth" (2:31–35).[3]

What are we to make of this strange dream? What is the hidden meaning in it? Most of the Jews suffering under Antiochus's persecution must have read into it the ultimate triumph of their God over the pagan tyrant who dared to challenge God by his savage acts of sacrilege and slaughter. They must have experienced tremendous psychological satisfaction and spiritual elation as they visualized the downfall of the world empires, especially the last and most hated Greek empire. To them the dream seemed to embody an apocalypse: the destruction of empires on earth was the apocalyptic manifestation of the power and glory of God's kingdom. Since there would be this apocalyptic victory of God on their behalf, they could endure with courage and hope the tyranny of the savage foreign ruler.

They were not the only ones who interpreted the dream in this way. Down the centuries, Christians in adverse socio-political situations have sought comfort, encouragement, and inspiration in the Book of Daniel.

But the dream and its interpretation contain meanings that go beyond the immediate concerns and hopes of Jews and Christians involved in struggle against diabolical socio-political forces. What we have here is in fact, to use Berdyaev's words again, "a design to history." As has been indicated, the story in the second chapter of Daniel is projected by a theology of history conceived in a particular situation: the Jews living in exile at the mercy of world powers. They lived between the times. The trauma of the exile was a thing of the past, but the future appears to them very uncertain. They have adjusted—with mixed success—to life in foreign lands, but they are caught up in power struggles of the empires. Their well-being and their destiny are closely linked with the outcome of such struggles.

The question of destiny is of course the question of history. History must therefore have become a subject of intense reflection for them. They have to reckon with the history of the nations as well as the history of their own nation. They must ponder deeply why and how their history has come to intersect with the history of other nations.

The first thing that strikes us in the second chapter of Daniel is that there the "design to history" is given a much wider basis than by Second Isaiah, who called Cyrus God's anointed. In his address to Nebuchadnezzar, before whom he was brought to interpret the dream, Daniel disclosed his fundamental understanding of "secular" kingly power in relation to the power of God. He said:

> You, O king, king of kings, to whom the God of heaven has given the kingdom with all its power, authority, and honor; in whose hands he has

placed men and beasts and birds of the air, wherever they dwell, grant-
ing you sovereignty over them all . . . [2:37–38].

With these elaborate words Daniel began the interpretation of the dream.

Even if we pass over the phrase "king of kings" as nothing more than the
Persian title for the monarch,[4] the rest of the address is formidable indeed.
Implied in it is the recognition that the power of the earthly kingdom comes
from God the creator. We must note that God here is not simply the God of
Israel but the God of heaven. In dealing with the nations, an enlarged vision
of God is necessary. The king who has conquered a vast territory in the ancient Near East calls for a God not defined by national or geographical
boundaries. That must be the reason why Daniel invokes the name of the
creator God. The history seen and projected in Daniel 2 is not just an extension of the history of Israel. Israel is not the basis or center of the history in
which a foreign nation has been playing a dominant role. History cannot be
explained by the centrism of Israel.

To understand the historical significance of a pagan king such as Nebuchadnezzar, we have to go all the way back to the creation. It is the God of
heaven, the God who created heaven and earth, and not just the God of
Israel, who has given King Nebuchadnezzar the power to conquer and rule.

The basic design of history is thus laid out in the creation. The meaning of a
nation cannot be derived simply from another nation. All nations must return to the creation to know how they are related to God and to one another.
This double relatedness is the clue to understanding God's design in history.
The God of history is the God of creation, and the God of creation is the God
of history. It is this God who has given into Nebuchadnezzar's hands "men
and beasts and birds of the air." Nebuchadnezzar's domain extends from
human society to the animal kingdom.

This seems to tell us that the theology of history in Daniel 2 goes beyond
that of Second Isaiah. By calling King Cyrus God's shepherd and loved one,
Second Isaiah already broke away from the view that regarded the national
and spiritual supremacy of Israel as central in the understanding of history.
This in itself was a great achievement. But for Second Isaiah it was essentially
a matter of introducing a foreign agent into the life and history of Israel.
Cyrus was to play an important role in the restoration of the temple in Jerusalem. But Nebuchadnezzar, the main human actor in the story of the dream
and its interpretation, brought not restoration but destruction to Jerusalem
and Judah. Here the theological mind behind the story must have undergone
a very curious turn.

True, it was not in Daniel 2 that the king hostile to Judah was first viewed in
a positive way. In fact it was Jeremiah who first called Nebuchadnezzar God's
servant. Jeremiah warned the people of Judah that God "will send for my
servant Nebuchadnezzar king of Babylon to punish them" (Jer. 25:9). Later,
after the fall of Jerusalem, Jeremiah, having been taken to Egypt against his

will, again warned that God "will send for my servant Nebuchadnezzar king of Babylon. . . . He will then proceed to strike Egypt" (Jer. 43:10).

But the passage that bears the closest relation to Daniel 2:37–38 is in Jeremiah 27, which carries the account of how Jeremiah tried to discourage an uprising against Nebuchadnezzar after the first sack of Jerusalem in 598 B.C. Shortly afterward Jeremiah, because of his counsel of surrender to the Babylonian king, was involved in a contest of prophecy with the false prophet Hananiah, who predicted a speedy restoration of peace to Jerusalem (Jer. 28).

What Jeremiah declared in the hearing of the king and the people is strikingly similar to Daniel's address to Nebuchadnezzar:

> I God made the earth with my great strength and with outstretched arm, I made man and beast on the face of the earth, and I give it to whom I see fit. I now give all these lands to my servant Nebuchadnezzar king of Babylon, and I give him also all the beasts of the field to serve him [Jer. 27:5–6].

For such a bold statement Jeremiah was treated as a traitor and nearly lost his life. But nothing could change his basic conviction that rebeling against Nebuchadnezzar is rebeling against Yahweh—this faith is the deepest ground for the prophet's action.

Two questions may be posed here. The first is: what compelled Jeremiah to call Nebuchadnezzar—the Babylonian king who had carried out the attacks on Jerusalem and taken the Jews into captivity—God's servant, a title never given to foreigners before? Without question this was against the national sentiment. More seriously it was a blunder of faith in the eyes of the overwhelming majority of the people.[5] Yet Jeremiah never wavered in his conviction, even in the face of opposition and threat to his life. It was a momentous decision of faith to make with regard to the enemy king.

How did he come to such a conclusion? Why did he have to act against the general feeling of the people? Perhaps his faith was never detached from his sensitivity to the history of the nations. Perhaps he realized that Israel's centrism could no longer solve its problems and relate it in a positive way to the political powers that rose and fell around it. There might have been other reasons that made him declare that Nebuchadnezzar was God's servant. In any case, he sensed that the time had come to wake his compatriots from the illusion of centrism, to challenge their faith in God's special dispensation for them at the cost of other nations and peoples, and to open their eyes to the wider horizon of history where new things were happening.

This leads to the second question: where do all histories get linked up and become intelligible in light of one another? For Jeremiah, as for the story in Daniel 2, that linkage is God's creative activity in the world. Jeremiah's specific reference to the creation of the earth, the animals, and human beings very much deserves our attention. He has to go back all the way to the creation to find the point that links all nations and their histories. There, in the creation, the power of a foreign ruler has its source.

Of course the legitimacy of power from its source does not guarantee the correct use of it. Something can always happen in the transition from divine power to human power. Power, though divine in origin, is corrupted when it is transferred to human beings. It happened to Nebuchadnezzar, whom Jeremiah called God's servant. It also happened to priests, kings, and people in Israel and Judah. It happened to all nations in the past; it happens to governments and their rulers today; it will also happen to those who will hold political, economic, and military power in the future.

The ethical problem of power is therefore a most difficult problem. It is no less an agonizing problem for God. The cross is where the power of God is rendered powerless by the power derived from God and held in the hands of political and religious authorities.

DECENTRALIZATION OF GOD'S POWER
IN WORLD HISTORY

To look upon Nebuchadnezzar as God's servant and to assert the centrism of Israel in the world are mutually exclusive. On the whole it can be said that, in contrast to the institutionalized religion that supported the political ideology of the kingdoms of Israel and Judah, the prophetic movement from Amos down to Isaiah was open to the decentralization of God's power in world history. This cannot, of course, be regarded as a consistent and systematic effort on the part of the prophets. In their critical view, Israel and Judah failed to live up to the love and justice expected of them—redemptive qualities they had experienced in the course of their history. It was profound disappointment at such failure that partly prompted the prophets to look elsewhere for signs and manifestations of God's presence in the world.

This must have been both a liberating and a painful experience. It was liberating because they overcame the perception of God as a tribal deity jealously guarding the interests of one particular nation and constantly at war with other nations as enemies and infidels. It was painful because they had to give up the long established notion that the claim of their nation to a privileged position in the sight of God could not be challenged.

Amos puts this experience most pointedly when he says:

> Are you Israelites not like Cushites to me?
>   says the Lord.
> Did I not bring Israel up from Egypt,
>   the Philistines from Caphtor,
>   the Arameans from Kir? [Amos 9:7]

This must have been a hard thing to say, even for an uncouth country farmer like Amos. Above all, it was an open challenge to the very basis of faith on which the socio-political and cultural-religious life of the nation had been constructed.

Centuries later, the religious leaders of Judaism were to hear an equally strong, if not stronger, challenge from a carpenter from Nazareth. Jesus said to the people: "Many, I tell you, will come from east and west to feast with Abraham, Isaac, and Jacob in the kingdom of Heaven. But those who were born to the kingdom will be driven out into the dark, the place of wailing and grinding of teeth" (Mt. 8:11–12). This must have outraged the religious leaders, for Jesus was clearly tampering with the religious faith centered on the notion of God's election. Jesus must have known what he was in for. His engagement with the religious leaders of his day went from challenge to polemic, from polemic to confrontation, and from confrontation to the tragedy of the cross. But the cross proved to be totally incompatible with a faith absolutized into a national religion. The community that gathered around Jesus was given new insights into the mystery of God's ways beyond itself as well as within itself.

Once centrism of Israel in history is broken, preferential treatment for Israel also has to go. This is Amos's conclusion. Can we call this the realism of prophetic theology? The people of Israel are not different to God from the Ethiopians, the Philistines, and the Arameans. If Israel is not the sole subject of God's saving love, other nations are not the sole objects of God's judgment either. The history of Israel, ridden with political and military setbacks, is an ample proof of this. Perhaps Amos has already foreseen a great debacle in the history of his own nation years later when the northern kingdom of Israel will be devastated by the powerful Assyrians. With much anguish he has to say this on behalf of God:

> Behold, I, the Lord God,
> have my eyes on this sinful kingdom,
> and I will wipe it off the face of the earth [Amos 9:8].

The political and religious leaders of Israel are enraged. Amaziah, the priest of the royal sanctuary at Bethel and the theological speaker for royal theology, issues a stern warning to Amos, ordering him to leave the country at once. "Be off, you seer!" He is white with rage: "Off with you to Judah! You can earn your living and do your prophesying there. But never prophesy again at Bethel, for this is the king's sanctuary, a royal palace" (Amos 7:12–13).

Let us not be naive. Decentralization of God's power is perceived by the ruling class as a threat to the centralization of political and religious power. The legitimacy of the latter is put to radical questioning. Decentralization of God's power is a prerequisite to learning how God is at work in Israel *and* in other nations. It also calls for a recognition of the power residing in the people within a nation. It poses a great threat for centralized power—both in politics and religion—in the hands of a few.

In Israel and Judah the threat developed into separation of prophetic theology from royal theology. The separation turned from time to time into open confrontation, as in the case of Amos and Amaziah. To use modern expressions, this is the confrontation between democracy and autocracy.

Centralization and decentralization of power—history is filled with struggles between these two. In a true sense, the cross symbolizes God's struggle against the centralization of the saving power of love in one nation and in one religion. Luke reports the risen Christ as saying to his disciples: ". . . the Messiah is to suffer death and to rise from the dead on the third day, and . . . in his name repentance bringing the forgiveness of sins is to be proclaimed to all nations" (Luke 24:46).

Jesus' death on the cross is the ultimate negation of human political and religious efforts to concentrate God's power in one particular community, race, or nation. God deals with all nations, not just Israel. God is engaged in the history of all nations, not just in the history of the Christian church. What does such awareness imply for Christian theology? It implies that Christian theology should also look *theologically* at the history of those nations that have remained outside the sphere of direct Christian influence. The arena of Christian theological activity has to be greatly expanded.

Decentralization of God's power among the nations does not, however, mean an unconditional sanction of power exercised by the nations. In fact it puts them in as critical a position as that of Israel and Judah in their relation with God. How could God, who did not spare Israel and Judah, become suddenly tolerant of the sins of the nations? If Israel and Judah are not immune from God's judgment, neither are the nations.

One of the most striking examples of this is found in Isaiah 10, where the prophet treats Assyria with both approval and denunciation. His outburst here was occasioned by the invasion of the Assyrian king Sennacherib in 701 B.C. to put an end to the coalition of Tyre, Ekron, Judah, and other west Palestinian states, with Hezekiah as its ringleader. Or it might have been Sennacherib's second invasion later in his reign, in 688 B.C. As a forceful spiritual leader, Isaiah played a critical role in these perilous hours of the nation.

Isaiah did not fail, even in that menacing situation, to see the invading foreign king in a positive light. Speaking for God, he had to say:

> The Assyrian! He is the rod
>   that I wield in my anger,
> and the staff of my wrath
>   is in his hand.
> I send him against a godless nation [Is. 10:5-6].

The notion that the nations can be God's instrument of punishment on Israel and Judah—a notion that would have disturbed the prophets in the classical period—is the beginning of the theology of history that has come to be expressed explicitly during the exilic period. It has to be said that the notion is not a conscious theological construct. It originated in a profoundly agonizing spirit, calling the nation of Israel to repentance.

Isaiah was saying in effect that true repentance consisted in recognizing the invading Assyrian forces as the instrument of God's punishment. This is surely no easy act of faith. How can one accept the invading enemy not with hatred and fear but with repentance? Is this not a kind of defeatism? Jeremiah, as we have seen, counseled Judah to surrender when the Babylonian army approached the city gates of Jerusalem. Why did these spiritual leaders seem to share a defeatist view in face of the invading enemy? Surrender was their advice. How could they be such wet blankets when the morale of the people had to be mobilized and their nerves toughened?

The prophets are not wet blankets. The hurt that their nation must sustain is their personal hurt. The disgrace that it has to go through is their personal disgrace too. They must have felt its defeat more painfully than others do. But for them the centrism of Israel in relation to God's work in history is over. The people of Israel must learn how God relates to other nations, even to the enemy nations.

The Assyrian king, however, exceeded the boundary set by God. He did not stop at being God's instrument of punishment; he took the opportunity to inflict excessive terror and brutality on Israel. Carried away by his victory, Sennacherib refused to recognize the power that was above him. The prophet was quick to point it out. Almost in the same breath as he spoke approvingly of the Assyrian king, he denounced him very harshly:

> But this man's purpose is lawless,
> lawless are the plans in his mind;
> for his thought is only to destroy
> and to wipe out nation after nation [Is. 10:7].

This was bad enough. But worse still, the ruthless Sennacherib credited all victories to his own power and was emboldened to pursue his territorial ambition without scruple. Because this was a betrayal of the divine commission, Assyria became the object of God's punishment.

Isaiah predicted that a miserable end was awaiting Sennacherib:

> Therefore the Lord, the Lord of Hosts,
> will send disease on his sturdy frame,
> from head to toe,
> and within his flesh
> a fever like fire shall burn [Is. 10:16].

Sennacherib could not escape God's judgment in spite of the fact that he was regarded as the divine agent to bring Israel to repentance.

Approval and judgment, acceptance and rejection—this paradox in God's dealings within history repeats itself both in Israel and in the nations. From the Christian point of view, history is the unfolding of this very paradox. The paradox discloses that decentralization is partly the way God exercises power. The prophets tried to drive this home to their complacent compatriots. Most of them had to suffer for it. And Jesus Christ acted out the paradox in his life and ministry. For this he too suffered, was rejected, and was put to death. The tragic fact is that the sacred cow of religious orthodoxy cannot be touched with impunity. But the cross was God's refusal to let the paradox dissolve in a monopoly of God's power by a privileged few.

A KINGDOM THAT FILLS THE WHOLE EARTH

After this rather long detour into the classical prophets, we must now return to the last part of Nebuchadnezzar's dream and its interpretation by Daniel. As King Nebuchadnezzar looked on in horror in his dream, an extraordinary stone from a mountain struck the statue and shattered it completely. But the destruction of the statue was not the end; it was not the signal to a return to the primordial chaos. It ushered in a new era of God's rule. As the story of the dream has it, the strange stone grew into a huge mountain, so huge that it practically filled the whole earth (Dan. 2:35).

What is this stone? According to Daniel's interpretation, the stone is an eternal kingdom to be established by God:

In the period of those kings, the God of heaven will establish a kingdom which shall never be destroyed; that kingdom shall never pass to another people; it shall shatter and make an end of all these kingdoms, while it shall itself endure for ever [2:44].

What sense can be made of this? What is the assumption hidden in its language, which, at first sight, has a strong eschatological overtone?

The central focus here is the stone that destroyed the statue, grew into a mountain, and became God's kingdom, in Daniel's interpretation. What interests us first about the stone is its origin. The stone was hewn from a mountain "not by human hands" (2:33). This implies that the stone was hewn by the divine hand. It was God who caused the stone to come into being and to perform the work of destruction. The stone was not self-motivated, but God-motivated. It was the manifestation of God's power, the embodiment of God's will.

The next thing that draws our attention is that the stone "was hewn from a mountain and grew into a mountain to fill the whole earth." The stone was hewn by the divine hand, true, but it did not have its origin in an otherworldly realm. It was a part of the earth and did its work within the earthly realm. It belonged to the world. It did its work within history.

This seems to mean further that the destruction of the four empires symbolized by the destruction of the statue does not lead to an obliteration of history. The stone did not make an apocalyptic end to the world, for the stone itself grew into a mountain and "filled the earth." Empires rise and fall; dynasties follow one after the other; life is born and disappears; history is made and disrupted. Outwardly, these are all human doings, but hidden in them is the seed of God's kingdom. At work in them is the creating and redeeming power of God. This is how the people of Israel viewed their history. This is the basis of their faith in God. This basic assumption of faith is now extended to other nations—in the strange episode we are considering here, to Babylon, to Media, to Persia, and to the Greek Empire.

The internal growth of God's kingdom within earthly kingdoms—this seems to be what the divine stone that comes from a mountain and fills the earth symbolizes. The kingdom of God is not an institution superimposed on the social and political institutions of this world.

As a matter of fact, it is misleading to render *malkoth* here "kingdom." *Malkoth* in the Old Testament, and its Greek equivalent *basileia* in the New Testament, should be translated "sovereignty"[6] or "reign"[7] of God. *Malkoth* or *basileia* is the power of God that acts within the powers and kingdoms of this world. It is the divine power that directs the course of history and judges empires and nations. The people of Israel accepted this into their faith and sought to express the power and reign of God in their historical experiences. Other nations might not have such a conscious faith. They had to be made aware of it. That is why Daniel's interpretation of the dream became a witness. It was a witness to the power and reign of God within history.

The impact of Daniel's witness must have been great, for the king was utterly overwhelmed. In astonishment he said to Daniel: "Truly, your God is indeed God of gods and Lord over kings" (2:47). Daniel's witness led to the king's confession. When such a confession is made, no matter where it is made and no matter who makes it, there and then the power of God becomes manifest and the reign of God is established. The reign of God therefore has no boundary. It is not defined by national borders or religious zones. It is not something that can be defined by our religious concepts and encompassed within our socio-political categories. The reign of God is something to which witness is given and to which confession is made.

We should bear this in mind when we hear Daniel say further: "That kingdom shall never pass to another people" (2:44). Since *malkoth* or *basileia,* the power and reign of God, is not a human possession, how can it be passed from one nation to another nation, one people to another people, as the result of a power struggle? Nor is it a hereditary right of one dynasty to pass it on to the next dynasty. Daniel's stress on the reign of God as "nontransferable" rules out the claim of a political leader or a political party to have a divine right to rule and govern from everlasting to everlasting. The power and reign of God is not a constitutional right of any ruling party. It simply cannot be constitutionalized.

A good and sound constitution bears a direct or indirect witness to the power and reign of God, but no politician can usurp it, not even by constitutional means. A president, a prime minister, or the secretary general of a ruling party can usurp the power and reign of God only be rewriting the constitution. But then that constitution loses at once its constitutionality. It forfeits its legitimacy and validity in the eyes of the people. The ruler who usurps God's power and reign by rewriting the nation's constitution loses "the Mandate of Heaven." This is true not only in the ancient world of monarchy but also in our world today. It is true for all times and all places.

God through Daniel, a captive Jew, brought the powerful Nebuchadnezzar to his knees. If that happened to the Babylonian king, how could it not also happen to Antiochus IV Epiphanes? This must have been one of the hidden motifs behind the compilation of the Book of Daniel. If God was seen at work in ancient Babylon in this way, why should God not be expected to act in a similar way again? This must be the secret hope of those Christians who read the Book of Daniel and maintain their faith in God as they struggle for freedom and justice under repressive socio-political forces.

But the story of Nebuchadnezzar's dream and its interpretation is not merely the story of how God takes revenge on the enemies of a harrassed people. It discloses to us the God who has a design of history for all nations and peoples.

Our theological task in Asia is to gain a glimpse of God's design for our part of the world. What we gain may not be more than just a fleeting glimpse, but that should be a very precious glimpse. It may lead us more deeply into the thoughts and ways of God with the people of Asia throughout the centuries.

GOD'S LORDSHIP OVER HISTORY

There is vitality in the way that some ancient prophets of Israel sought to relate their nation to other nations. There is a remarkable openness in the way they tried to comprehend the work of God in history. Has the Christian church today shown such vitality, as the world around it undergoes radical change? Has Christian theology demonstrated such openness when other religions and cultures clamor for the attention of the world? Or has theology largely remained captive to its own thought-forms and engrossed in its traditional problem-solving process? Has it continued to engage in a domestic colloquy that has little hope of gaining a hearing from those outside the Christian community?

One should not attempt a simple and general answer for any of these questions. But they do carry a certain urgent note in them. The sense of urgency that these questions project is heightened as we listen to some statistics on the kind of world we as Christians share with the rest of humankind.

One fourth of the world population professes the Christian faith. *Three fourths* of the world population profess other faiths or adhere to a secular conviction. And given the geographical spread of that division,

it is likely that by the year 2000, less than *one fifth* of the world population will be Christian.[8]

Most Christians must be at least vaguely aware of the distribution of the
world religious population mentioned here. But put in such cold statistics the
situation may give those Christians who still live on the legacy of Christian
culture a sense of shock and disbelief. In the United States, for example,
coins and dollar bills still bear the words: "In God we trust." Britons stand
respectfully at attention when the national anthem "God Save the Queen" is
played. And in some countries on the continent of Europe such as West Germany, Sweden, and Norway, the phrase "state church" has not yet become
obsolete.

According to *The Britannica Book of the Year 1978,* the number of Christians in Asia—Roman Catholic, Orthodox, and Protestant—is close to 90
million, Buddhists more than 260 million, Hindus 515 million, Muslims 433
million. In Africa, the Muslim population is almost as large as the Christian
population (134 million Muslims, 137 million Christians). Furthermore, "almost 35% of the world's population do not profess a religious faith but either
adhere to a secular ideology or profess no conviction at all."[9] If we take China
into consideration, we have a very disturbing picture. There 900 million persons—an informed demography suggests one billion—are under a political
and ideological system that regards religion as a reactionary element contra-
dictory to the socialist reconstruction of the nation.

For us Christians this situation is a cause for concern. It puts into question
some basic assumptions of the Christian faith. In what sense is God the Lord
of history? How should we think of God's relation to the great part of the
world's population that does not profess the Christian faith? Are *all* people
saved only through Jesus Christ? But what is salvation? How is it related to
the struggle of the poor, the oppressed, the homeless, the majority of whom
are beyond the pale of Christianity?

Other factors add to our perplexity. We have often been told that in the very
countries where the life and history of the people have been shaped under the
influence of Christianity the church has been pushed out of the decision-
making center, largely by the force of secularization. There are some hard
facts to support the contention of the "decline" of traditional Christianity in
the West. In his study *Religion in Secular Society,* the English sociologist
Bryan Wilson discloses some chilling statistics. His study shows that there
has been "a steady diminution in the proportion of people who go to church
in European countries, and particularly so in the Protestant countries.
Average Sunday attendance is as low as less than three percent of the population in Norway, and between ten to fifteen percent in England. . . ."[10]

Of course the health of Christianity cannot be judged merely by church
attendance on Sunday. It can be argued that under the surface of indifference
to the church there are strong undercurrents of Christian spirituality at work
in society. Particularly in times of crisis and upheaval, that spirituality asserts

itself in prophetic voices, acts as the light of hope to the people in confusion and despair, and shapes the human spirit to move into the future. It is, however, true that the strong influence the church used to have in education, community life, and politics has waned. The church as an institution has little direct impact on matters of national policy.

In contrast, Islam, for instance, holds a prominent place in a Muslim country. It is a decisive factor in the socio-political affairs of the nation. The revolution, under Islamic leaders, that destroyed the powerful monarchy of the shah in Iran is a striking proof of the power that Islam has woven into the fabric of that nation. India in principle is a secular state, but we all know how Hinduism is still a powerful factor that exerts great influence on the nation in every way. Even in the case of Buddhism, regarded stereotypically as a world-denying religion, there is the curious example of Burma where it holds a prominent place in "the Burmese way to socialism." It is in this kind of world—from the First to the Third World—that Christians in East and West have to relearn their faith and ponder deeply the ways of God with the nations. We need a theology that is different from the theology manufactured in the ivory tower of so-called Christendom.

Arend van Leeuwen's book *Christianity in World History*[11] is one of the few serious theological attempts in this direction. The title of the book itself is suggestive. It places Christianity in the context of the whole world. It aims at redefining the role of Christianity in the postcolonial era. It searches for ways in which Christianity can become a positive force in the future of world culture. Altogether, it is a laudable effort that has vividly brought to the minds of thinking Christians in both East and West the new missionary task of the church in a radically changed world.

But the book has a serious flaw. Van Leeuwen, a Dutch theologian, discourses, argues, and envisions with the centrism of Israel and Christianity as the controlling factor. In his theological exposition of the relation between Israel and the nations, he gives a clear expression to such centrism. As he sees it:

> Israel and the land of Israel represent the whole earth, the whole of mankind. Israel herself is a new creation, and her land the token of a new earth which the Lord will create. For that reason the life of the whole earth hangs upon the promise that Israel is to return to her land. . . . The Lord reveals by Israel, his people, what his purpose is for the whole earth.[12]

It is true that there is this strong centric thinking in the Old Testament, but it is also true that there have been efforts to break out of it to understand Israel and the nations in a relation of mutuality. For van Leeuwen these efforts seem nonexistent. Is it because of this that Cyrus, the Persian king, and Nebuchadnezzar, the Babylonian king, receive only passing remarks in his book?

In van Leeuwen's theology, the centrism of Israel is developed into the centrism of Christianity. For him this is logical. God begins with the church and returns to the church. The church is God's *terminus a quo* and also *terminus ad quem*. Although van Lueewen does not tell us what he means by "church," clearly it is the church that has developed in the course of the past two thousand years that he is referring to. But Israel as a historical and political entity in the Old Testament ceased to exist, and there is no guarantee that the church as a historical institution will endure unchanged. It is therefore difficult to know what it means for Israel and the Christian church to represent the whole of humanity. This is the point where a theological assertion must answer the question of historical realism. We cannot let it hang in mid-air, leaving it without any historical reference.

Christian theology has always prided itself on taking history seriously. God is the God of history. God works in history and is the Lord of history. Unlike Hinduism, which cares little for history, the Christian faith is a historical faith.

History is one of the most important trademarks of Christian theology. It is then certainly not untheological to ask what the history of China means in God's salvation. Nor is it untheological to ask what God's will for the world is in the realignment of international political powers in this postcolonial era.

We as Christians should not too readily claim a representative role for Israel or for Christianity without first making theological investigations into the historical experiences of the nations and peoples outside the Jewish and Christian traditions. The validity of theological assertions of faith must be tested and challenged by historical realities to which our life and faith are closely related. Historical realism calls for theological realism. The rigor of historical realism will, I am sure, enable us Christians to face gut issues of life and history with our faith not only challenged but also deepened and enriched.

It must be said that van Leeuwen, despite his Christian centrism, is aware of the importance for Christians to become better informed about other cultures and religions. He stresses that Christians should join with the peoples of other religions and cultures and work with them. He speaks of the need to discover the treasures in the traditions of other peoples and to make "free and proper use of the rich stores of wisdom and experience deposited within the history of African and Asian cultures."[13] He is not halfhearted about his advice, for he goes on to say:

> Here are opportunities in inexhaustible abundance for the Christians to steep themselves no less completely than their non-Christian fellows and compatriots in the values, spiritual and material, social and individual, philosophical, political and economic, of the non-Western civilizations.[14]

Whether such advice is achieveable or not is beside the point. It is imperative that Christians no longer remain in utter ignorance of what other persons believe and practice. Christian assertions of faith should not be made in ignorance of what has been happening in the broader human community. But for van Leeuwen the effort involves much more than the self-education of Christians. He has an aggressive goal in view when he concludes by saying: "In that way, a Christian can make as vital a contribution to the renewal of Islamic or of Indian civilization as any Muslim or Hindu."[15] This is a big order for Christians! Van Leeuwen seems to be advocating that Islam or Hinduism not only need Muslim or Hindu reformers but also Christian reformers for its renewal.

The spirit of understanding and involvement expressed here should certainly be commended. One must not take it lightly. But the weakness of his Christian centrism shows particularly at two points. First, if Islam needed Christians for its renewal, has it ever occurred to van Leeuwen that perhaps Christianity too might need Muslims for its own renewal? The guess is that this has not struck him as a real possibility. He gives us a vision of going to other cultures and religions, reforming and renewing them. But he does not seem to entertain the idea that traffic in the opposite direction could also be a possibility, at least in theory. Christianity can take care of itself as well as others.

The next point we want to raise is this: the traditional concept of *Heilsgeschichte* seems to be the guiding principle of van Leeuwen's theology. This becomes evident when he says toward the end of his book: "In this age of ours 'Christianization' can only mean that peoples become involved in the onward movement of Christian history."[16] Coming from a theologian who knows a great deal about the changed and changing world of politics, cultures, and religions, the statement is somewhat surprising. How can we expect a practicing Buddhist, for instance, to join "the onward movement of Christian history" without giving up his or her faith and culture? How is it possible for a Hindu to become "involved" in it without ceasing to be a Hindu? Does van Leeuwen have in mind a kind of Christian history that sums up commendable elements in the other religions? Or does he believe that the world will be "Christianized" some day?

Whatever answers van Leeuwen may give to these questions, it seems clear that for him Christianity constitutes the most dominant force in world history. What Christianity is and represents has been decisive for almost two thousand years especially in the western part of the world. Although he concedes that the influence of Christianity—in its traditional form—on the world has declined, he believes that it is reappearing in different ways. As he puts it: "Although the period of Western domination is ending, the impact of Western civilization on the non-Western world has only just entered the first stage. What does that involve for the history of the Church?"[17] He is referring here to the forces of western secularization that have been bringing science, technology, democracy, freedom, and the like, to Third World nations. The world, East and West, is becoming secularized. This is true. Would this also mean westernization of Buddhist faith or Hindu religious practices? Would this lead to the replacement of indigenous cultural heritages by the "secular-ized" civilization of the West? One hesitates to give a positive answer to these questions.

What seems to be happening in many Third World countries is that secular-ization has not put an end to the renaissance of indigenous culture. Bread, to give a simple example, has become an important family food item in some countries in Asia. It is a convenient food, a fast food. It is ready on the breakfast table to be eaten when you struggle out of bed early in the morning. In five or ten minutes you finish your breakfast and are ready to take to the road. There is no washing of rice, putting it on the fire, waiting for half an hour for it to be cooked. Bread is a symbol of western efficiency. It brings the reality of western civilization to the kitchen and dining room. It has to some extent changed the eating habits of a great number of Asians. In spite of all this, bread has not replaced rice as the staple food of the people. When Asians think of food, they think of rice, not bread. When they talk about food, they talk about rice, not bread. When they are hungry, they ask for rice, not bread.

In the midst of "the onward movement" of secularized western civilization in the East, rice civilization has not been replaced by bread civilization. Al-though the Asian mind is often viewed by the western philosophical mind as "syncretistic" or "eclectic," when it comes to crucial matters such as food and culture, it knows what its choice must be. The mind, soul, spirit, and body, nourished and cultivated by rice, will not become less "Asian" because of the adoption of bread into dietary habits. Rice culture flourishes.

If this metaphor of rice and bread sounds a little preposterous, there is a more serious issue to be addressed. Van Leeuwen believes that the impact of secularized western civilization on the Third World will continue to increase and expand. He may be right in this. But he seems to imply that the Christian church should be on the heels of that civilization, carrying out its own mis-sion in the "non-Western" world.

Is this not a false strategy? Christians in the Third World have been put on the defensive precisely on this question of the relation between the gospel and western culture. Enlightened Christians in both East and West have been saying for some time that the marriage between the Christian gospel and the western gunboats was a marriage of convenience and should have ended in divorce as soon as possible. But van Leeuwen seems to be suggesting a similar strategy, although in a different form and in a different spirit. We cannot help asking: why should the gospel of salvation follow the lead of "secularized" western culture when many of its values and criteria have increasingly come to be questioned and contested? Why should the gospel have to be preached as if it always needed the company of a western bodyguard?

Perhaps there is a final point to add. It must have been due to his centrism of Israel and Christianity that van Leeuwen was prevented from looking into *theo*-logical meanings of the Asian cultures and religions discussed by him in his book. Has God not been active in these cultures and histories? Is it impos-sible for Christians to find God's footsteps in them? In what ways are these footsteps related to God's footsteps that we clearly see in the history of Israel and in the history of the Christian church? Are they of a similar kind? Or are they totally different?

Oriental theologians are not just orientalists. Their main concern should be related to the question of how God is involved in the life and history of the nations beyond the orbit of the Christian church. God has written history with the people of Israel. God has written and is still writing history with the Christian church. But God as the creator and redeemer must have also been writing history with the people of Malaysia, China, Japan, and Taiwan. How does this history get written? This is a question for Christian theologians, especially for Third World theologians.

Transpositional theology has to continue its work. It has to chart its course following the traces of the past and taking some calculated risks. That is why we have tried, in this part of our study, to see how God developed the plot of history with Israel and with its neighboring nations. Our attempt has given us some fresh insights and some new perspectives. But this is just a beginning. We must go on to the center of our faith—Jesus Christ—and see what insight and what vision he can give us to deepen our understanding of God's ways with *all* people. We will now turn to Jesus Christ in the next part of our exploration.

Part II

THE GREAT DISRUPTION

Then Jesus replied:
"In truth,
  in very truth I tell you,
  a grain of wheat
  remains a solitary grain
  unless it falls into the ground
  and dies.
But if it dies,
  it bears a rich harvest"
              [John 12:23–24].

CHAPTER FOUR

Beginning at the End

Let us begin at the end, for the end often throws a new light on the beginning. This is particularly true concerning Jesus Christ. It is common knowledge that the faith of the earliest Christian community was centered in the cross and resurrection of Jesus Christ. The New Testament itself, in fact, was very much the product of the post-Easter experiences of the disciples and apostles.[1]

In Jesus we have to do with a very special person for whom the end is the beginning. His end on the cross transformed by the resurrection becomes the beginning of the faith that is capable of "turning the world upside down" (Acts 17:6; RSV). It is this faith born out of the cross-resurrection that produces echoes in the Gospels, vibrates in the Acts of the Apostles, gushes forth in the Pauline letters, and permeates the rest of the New Testament.

Jesus at the end of his ministry is projected back to the beginning as lying in a manger attracting attention from a few humble shepherds. He is also projected forward to the end of time as the king of glory who will bring his mission to its fulfillment. His end is his new beginning with God, with humanity, and with the whole creation. That is why his end is where we must begin.

DEATH OF AN EXPECTED MESSIAH

What an end and what a beginning that is! The cross blasted the portentous atmosphere surrounding his alleged messiahship. Everyone was affected, each in a different way. There were, first of all, those resistance fighters called Zealots, who fought to overthrow the Roman imperial rule by force.[2] Even Jesus seemed to have secretly sympathized with them. During his ministry, he "found himself in a certain sense close to the Zealots," and "there was for him a Zealotist temptation."[3] The cross must, therefore, have been all the more bitter a disappointment for them.

There was also the crowd of followers who must have shared the political aspirations of the Zealots. They had welcomed Jesus to Jerusalem as their expected king and messiah. They shouted at the top of their voices: "Hosanna to the Son of David! Blessings on him who comes in the name of the Lord! Hosanna in the heavens!" (Mt. 21:9) But a messiah of their expectations Jesus was not to be. Instigated by their religious leaders, this same crowd of persons who had earlier shouted Hosanna was to ask Pilate for the release of Barabbas and to demand Jesus' execution.

Even the disciples were not above the misguided enthusiasm for their teacher. According to Luke's Gospel, it was they who led the crowd in a chorus of acclamation as Jesus entered Jerusalem on the colt: "Blessings on him who comes as king in the name of the Lord! Peace in heaven, glory in highest heaven!" (Lk. 19:38).

Jesus himself, for a moment, must have been caught in a sea of fanaticism, for as some Pharisees asked him to restrain his disciples, he replied: "I tell you, if my disciples keep silence the stones will shout aloud" (Lk. 19:40). But when Jesus was led to the cross, the disciples fled, leaving their master to endure the final hours of agony.

And of course the religious and political authorities were watching the whole development with great apprehension and misgiving. True, among the Pharisees there were persons like Nicodemus who courageously defended Jesus. To his colleagues intent on doing Jesus in, Nicodemus protested: "Does our law permit us to pass judgment on a man unless we have first given him a hearing and learned the facts?" (Jn. 7:51) But in the end the hostile elements won out and Jesus was brought to Pontius Pilate, the Roman procurator, to be tried and executed as a political offender.

Pilate, for his part, was not sure whether he should comply with the Jewish religious authorities. He tried, in his own way, to dismiss the case, but finally succumbed to the mounting frenzy of his colonial subjects. All that he was able to do was to wash his hands and declare: "My hands are clean of Jesus' blood; see to that yourselves" (Mt. 27:24). But he too was not innocent of Jesus' blood, for it was he who, despite having the authority to release Jesus, handed him over to his soldiers to be crucified.

From the very beginning the Christian faith has to reckon with Jesus' death on the cross. What an inauspicious beginning! Death is a disruption of life—an irrevocable disruption. Death negates life, conquers meaning, and destroys the relationships that make life possible. Death puts an end to being human and personal. And Jesus' death was not an ordinary death; it was an ignominious death on the horrible cross. It was a mockery of all his teachings about goodness and beauty. It made nonsense of his discourse on life—eternal life. It put an end to the hope for the coming of God's kingdom on earth. The death on the cross was an absolute death. It was an abolition of hope. It was a negation of values held in the religious traditions of his people.

What is more, Jesus' death on the cross was not merely the death of a private person. To the great disillusionment of many, his death was that of an expected messiah. Here something more than just the life of an individual person was destroyed. At stake was the life of a nation that had never given up its expectation of a political messiah from the house of David. Who else could that messiah be except Jesus who was "son of David and son of Abraham" (Mt. 1:1)? Where else could they find their prospective leader except in Jesus who "taught with a note of authority" (Mt. 7:29)? Who could have been their liberator but the one who dared to challenge Herod the king, saying: "Go and tell that fox, 'Listen: today and tomorrow and the next day I shall be casting out devils and working cures; on the third day I reach my goal' " (Lk. 13:32)? Jesus' death on the cross was literally a nightmare, a bad dream, from which one woke up trying hard to forget. The one last hope of restoring Israel to its ancient glory was dashed to the ground. The kingdom that might have been able to claim continuity with the house of David crumbled.

Once again God seemed to be making a fool of Israel. God did not seem to be playing their game. For God the unbroken existence of Israel as a messianic nation did not seem to matter. The death of an expected messiah—this was the only way the ardent followers of Jesus could view his death. His contemporaries were not able to rise above their nationalistic goal to perceive the meaning of the great disruption brought about by Jesus' death. To them Jesus' death was a supreme tragedy. The God who allowed their messianic hope to be crucified on the cross must be a tragic God. St. Paul said it most pointedly: "Christ nailed to the cross . . . is a stumbling block to Jews" (1 Cor. 1:25).

But as T. W. Manson, a British New Testament scholar, has shrewdly observed: "the Jewish hope of a successful Messiah was equally a stumbling block to Jesus."[4] He goes on to say: "It is from this point of view of the fundamental contradiction between the Jewish Messianic hope and Jesus' convictions concerning his own Ministry that the Gospel becomes, in its main lines, an intelligible piece of history."[5] The key phrase here is "the fundamental contradiction." Jesus' death on the cross contradicted radically and fundamentally the faith and ethos of the Jewish community handed down from one generation to the next from the time of the patriarchs to the time of Jesus Christ.

It was a formidable tradition to contradict. It was a tenacious religious system to challenge. It was a stubborn continuity to break. A successful messiah, to use Manson's phrase, would have affirmed that tradition. He would have upheld that religious system. He would have extolled that continuity. And in doing so, he would have negated God's saving love for all humankind. An enormous struggle must have gone on within this contradiction. Even Jesus' most trusted disciple Peter tried to disuade him from contradicting the Jewish hope of a successful messiah (see Mk. 8:31–33; Mt. 16:21–23). The pressures from all quarters on Jesus to accept the role of a successful messiah must have been tremendous. The story of the temptation alone testifies to this (Mt. 4:1–10; see Lk. 4:1–12). The contradiction must have almost consumed Jesus with its intensity.

The death of an expected messiah put an end to that contradiction. The cross was the pronouncement of God's verdict on the politico-religious traditions of messianic hope in Israel. Through the painful cross God declared that Jesus Christ was not the expected messiah of the Jewish people. The fact that the cross became a stumbling block to Jews even more forcefully dissociated Jesus from the nationalistic messianism of his compatriots. The cross tragically but dramatically demonstrated that God would not have anything to do with the messianism bred in nationalism. It made painfully clear that a national messiah, if there was to be one, had to be sought somewhere else.

Thus on the cross Jesus became uprooted from his own race, his own nation, his own religion. His disciples forsook him and ran away. Peter denied him vigorously and dissociated himself from him. He was abandoned as a messiah who had aborted the great national cause, who had not lived up to the national expectation. The religious leaders disowned him completely, putting to rest his alleged pretension to the Jewish throne.

His uprootedness went even further: he was also uprooted from God. By abandoning him on the cross, God let it be known that Jesus was not commissioned to be a messiah in the line of David. God dealt a deathblow to any lingering illusion about Jesus as a possible national leader. The sharp cry of Jesus on the cross was the cry of this uprootedness from God: "My God, my God, why hast thou forsaken me?" (Mk. 15:34; Mt. 27:46) Forsaken both by God and by his own people, Jesus experienced disruption with the history of his nation and with the politico-religious aspirations of his own people.

This great disruption caused by Jesus' death on the cross should lead to a radical reorientation in the thinking of the church concerning God's engagement with the world. If the cross is a negation of Jewish messianism, it should also be a negation of Christian messianism, the messianism that believed in the Christian church and its history as the sole instrument of God's saving work in the world. Such Christian messianism makes it impossible for Christians to experience God outside the Christian community.

To speak of God at work outside the history and culture deeply affected by Christianity becomes very difficult. God is the God of Christians, but not of Hindus. God has everything to do with Christian culture but has hardly anything to do with Buddhist culture. Christian messianism becomes the guiding principle by which Christian thinkers view the world and history, just as messianism was normative for the royal theology in ancient Israel. This is the main reason why the church and its theology have been unable to make "redemptive" sense out of historical experiences and cultural traditions of peoples apart from the western world. The great disruption in history caused by the death of an expected messiah is thus essential for our experience of God outside the boundary of Christianity.

JESUS IN THE WOMB OF DARKNESS

The death of an expected messiah was accompanied by some powerful portents. To realize the force of the great disruption that Jesus' death has caused, we must turn to these portents and ponder what they might mean.

There was, first of all, the darkness that enveloped the whole land in the middle of the day. As Matthew's Gospel tells us: "From midday a darkness fell over the whole land, which lasted until three in the afternoon" (27:45; see Mk. 15:33; Lk. 23:44). Darkness is associated with fear. In darkness lurks danger. Caught in darkness we become panicky and grope for a ray of light. There is much unknown in darkness. Our faculty to sense, to see, and to discern becomes severely restricted. We find ourselves at its mercy.

This is the kind of darkness that descended on the Egyptian soldiers in pursuit of Hebrew slaves, threw them into confusion, and brought them to defeat (Ex. 10:21–28). To the Egyptians darkness was God's judgment. Similarly Amos speaks of "God darkening the earth in broad daylight, turning pilgrim-feasts into mourning and songs into lamentation" (Amos 8:9).[6]

But the darkness that fell on the whole land in broad daylight from noon until three o'clock on Good Friday was something entirely different. It had to be something different, because a disruption of a tremendous magnitude was about to occur, involving not only Jerusalem and Judea, but the whole earth. It could not be a darkness to provide cover for Jesus' disciples to escape the clutch of the religious authorities. Nor could it be a darkness in which God would wreak vengeance upon those who conspired to have Jesus nailed to the cross. The darkness at the threshold of this great disruption was neither a protection for Jesus' followers nor God's vengeance on those who engineered Jesus' death. It was the darkness from which a new light would shine, a new day would break, and a new experience of God's saving work would become possible.

In haste we must stretch our imagination to the darkness that covered the face of the abyss at the begining of the creation in Genesis 1. There God was in the darkness, worked in that darkness, and brought the creation out of that darkness. This is the darkness of the womb in which a new life is created and developed for the day of birth. In that darkness is spawned the mystery of nothing becoming everything, of emptiness growing into fullness, and of chaos yielding to creation. God's creation takes place while the whole universe is shrouded in utter darkness.

Just before Jesus' death took place on the cross, the whole land, we are told, was covered with darkness. This was not an accident. The darkness at this critical hour signaled the end of the chapter on an expected messiah for Israel. A totally different messiah was about to emerge from the darkness, opening a new chapter of God's saving work in history. The pitch darkness that covered the whole land for three hours forcefully separated the new chapter from the old chapter. It broke the continuity of the story in which a messiah for Israel played the principal role. It introduced the story in which nations other than Israel are also prominent characters. On the cross shrouded in darkness an expected messiah of Israel was being transformed into the prototype of a messiah for peoples and nations in search of redemptive meaning in their own history and in their own community.

A new kind of creation was taking place in that darkness—a kind of creation that would free God's salvation from Jewish captivity, release God's redeeming power in human community, and reshape the world through the sweat and blood of peoples struggling for freedom and love against all manner of social and political odds. It was the darkness of pangs before the dawn of birth. A tremendous birthpang was taking place in that sudden darkness. In the midst of that darkness stood the cross as the symbol and reality of that pain of birth. The cross was the word of God uttered in pain and in hope. It summed up the sufferings and longings of all human beings since the beginning of time. The cross that stood at the center of the darkness, that womb of creation, embraces all the crosses that humanity has had to bear throughout history.

The powerful and pregnant silence of the darkness, however, was broken, according to Mark's and Matthew's Gospels, by the heartrending cry of Jesus: "My God, my God, why hast thou forsaken me?"[7] As has been mentioned, this cry makes definitive Jesus' disruption with the religio-political expectations of his own people. When the veil of darkness was lifted, the world was confronted with the fact that Jesus was *not* the political messiah of the Jewish people.

As a matter of fact, expectation in Jesus and suspicion of him as an expected messiah lingered around the person of Jesus even as he was hanging on the cross. At the crucified Jesus both the crowd and religious leaders hurled abusive words, taunting him to come down from the cross and save himself. Jesus had to bear the pain of these taunts as well as the pain of the cross. To be anything else than an expected messiah was such a frightfully difficult thing. But Jesus' cry of dereliction was decisive. Even God counted him out as a possible political savior for the oppressed Jewish nation. Jesus was not going to be a second Moses leading his people out of the hand of their political oppressor. There was not going to be a second exodus to be celebrated with songs and dancing. Instead, Jesus as an expected messiah must die.

The hideous cross instituted for the execution of political offenders by the Roman regime put an end once and for all to any illusion about Jesus as a national messiah. The cross was God's verdict on the "messianic" community obsessed with an exclusive messianic dream in contradiction to God's purpose of salvation for the whole of humanity. In Jesus on the cross the tension between the history of a particular nation, conscious of a special place in God's providence, and the history of all nations, unaware of God's saving presence among them, reached a breaking point. Jesus on the cross was forsaken even by God as a would-be national messiah, but reaffirmed as the savior whose redemptive significance reached beyond the borders of Jewish historical and cultural experiences.

THE CURTAIN TORN IN TWO

Jesus died, abandoned by God and by his own religious community. But, in contrast to the deep silence of complete darkness that had preceded his death "there was," in the words of Matthew's Gospel, "an earthquake" (27:51). The earth shook with the agony of Jesus' death. It could not contain the oppressive silence surrounding the cross. It could not receive meekly and silently the death of Jesus, the death that was to mark a momentous change in history. The earth mourned and quaked.

Another portent followed. "The curtain of the temple," to quote Mark's Gospel, "was torn in two from top to bottom" (15:38; see Mt. 27:51). What kind of sign might this be? What did it symbolize? What was it pointing to?

An interesting and insightful explanation of the symbolism of the curtain that was torn in two when Jesus died is given by Pierre Benôit, a French biblical scholar:

> The veil is a symbol which stands for the barrier which kept pagans away from the Jewish religion. The veil in question is probably that of the Holy Place, rather than that of the Holy of Holies; it hid the interior of the Temple from people in the outer court, above all from pagans; and by excluding them it protected the private mystery of the religion, the intimate presence of Yahweh inside the Temple. For the veil to be torn meant that the privacy and exclusiveness were abolished, and so Jewish worship ceased to be the privilege of a single people and access to it became open to all, even to Gentiles. Such is the deeper meaning of this phenomenon.[8]

This explanation suggests that here is a no less portentous sign than that of the darkness that covered the whole earth before Jesus' death. In fact the temple curtain torn in two at Jesus' death should be a momentous point of departure for our transpositional theology.

The most crucial element in this symbolism is the veil. This is of course no ordinary veil made of flimsy material. "The veil of the Temple," says Benôit, "was heavier than a Bedouin tent."[9] A Bedouin tent must be strong enough to withstand the rigor of desert life. It protects the Bedouins from the scorching sun and the merciless gusts of sand and wind during the daytime. It provides them with a shelter from frost and wild animals during the dark hours of night. It is their castle in the desert. It is their fortress against the intrusion of inhospitable elements. It is their security as they trudge along in the hostile and unpredictable world of sand and heat. A Bedouin tent tells the story of Bedouin life. It has to be heavy, strong, and reliable. It has to be waterproof, heatproof, frostproof, and, above all, enemyproof.

The veil of the Temple was heavier and stronger than a Bedouin tent. Why did the Temple need such a veil? The Temple did not have to fear heat, frost, or rain, for it was built with stone on a solid foundation. But just as a Bedouin tent was the center of Bedouin life, so the Temple was the center of the life and worship of the Jewish people. The Temple was the religious and political history of the Jewish nation. And above all, the Temple cultivated, protected, and harbored a "messianic secret" that could not be shared by outsiders.

It was this messianic secret that had to be guarded with utmost care. That secret had to be hidden from the eyes of the impious. It had to be kept from the intrusion of pagans. That is why a thick and heavy veil had to be installed between the interior of the Temple and the outer court—the interior where the messianic secret was closely guarded by priests and the faithful, and the outer court where the unworthy ones such as women and children, and especially pagans, strained their neck in vain for a glimpse of the mystery to which they had no access. The veil of the Temple had to be heavy enough to resist the penetration of a curious eye. It had to be thick enough to discourage the intrusion of an aspiring heart. It had to be strong enough to hold at bay the cries and shouts of those gripped by fear, frustration, and uncertainty. It had to be heavier than the already heavy Bedouin tent.

It is this veil of the Temple that was torn in two from top to bottom at the death of Jesus. It was not a halfhearted mediocre tear. The tear was complete: the veil split into two pieces. It did not tear apologetically or reluctantly; it tore swiftly, abruptly, and at one breath. The tear of the curtain was decisive and final. It could not be patched or repaired; it had to be left torn open.

This was an extraordinary happening. In the long history of Israel, there must have been attempts to make an opening, just a small opening, in this heavy curtain of the Temple. The prophets of the Old Testament did it with varied degrees of success. There must have been religious reformers within Judaism who tried to make a little hole in the curtain. But the curtain was so formidable that it had successfully resisted many assaults. And even as Jesus was struggling with God and humanity on the painful cross, this curtain stood invincibly between the mystery of Jewish religion and the people denied access to it. But the time for the invincible curtain ran out. It withstood everything in the course of its long history, but one thing it finally failed to withstand—the death of Jesus. At the death of Jesus, the curtain of the Temple was torn in two from top to bottom.

The death of Jesus is *not* the death of God. On the contrary, it shows to the world how alive God is, how actively God is involved in the saving work, and how vigorously God is engaged with human beings in their agony and suffering. The death of Jesus brings God close to the world—as close as God can be. It also makes God's presence in us real—as real as God can possibly be. The death of Jesus is the fulfillment of Immanuel, God-with-us, God-with-all-humanity, God-with-all-creation. God-with-all-nations-and-with-all-peoples is the meaning of the Word become flesh.

That is why the curtain of the Temple must be torn apart and removed. God had not been working behind the curtain separated from persons outside an institutionalized religion. God was not hiding behind the veil worried about public overexposure. Instead, there in the place of a skull, in the full view of all, God was fully exposed in all weakness and agony. God did not need the protection of the thick veil in the past and certainly will not need it in the future.

The ruptured curtain made an end to a God wrapped in a cloak of mystery, ensconced in the darkness of the Holy Place, and inaccessible to children, women, peasants, workers, prostitutes, and pagans. It abolished the barriers that had for so long separated the God of Israel from the God of the nations. The death of Jesus, which tore open the curtain of the Temple, could now be linked to the despair and hope, suffering and joy, death and life, of the millions and millions of persons who pass through the world from the beginning to the end of time. The ruptured veil is the symbol of hope for those who have had to wait patiently and desperately in the outer court for such a long time for God's saving words for them.

The sundered curtain of the Temple must be a crisis for a religion that, through misguided zeal, seeks to turn God into a privileged possession of a particular nation or religious community. When the curtain of the Temple was torn open, many must have discovered, to their horror and chagrin, that that most sacred shrine of their piety, believed to be filled with the full presence of God, was empty. God was not there where their religion had taught them God was. Instead, God was out there in an open place on the hill where the cruel cross was standing. This God in Jesus Christ must have taken them by surprise. And for the religious authorities the consternation must have been painful. They lost their privileges that came from a secluded God. Their pretension was shaken because an empty Holy Place made their religious taboos against the underprivileged and pagans unjustifiable.

The death of Jesus on the cross is a judgment not only on the sin of the world, but on a religion that hides God from people, misrepresenting God to them, and erecting barriers between the saved and the unsaved, between the godly and the ungodly. A religion that measures the depth, breadth and width of God's saving love by the measure of its own traditions, orthodoxy, and laws comes under the scrutiny of the cross. The death of Jesus turns a religion inside out. It deals a blow to those bent on reducing God to a measurable size, doing their utmost to keep God from getting out of their hand, and holding God captive to their rigid theological framework.

Religion, as a matter of fact, often tends to underestimate the power of its God. It fails to realize that it cannot set a limit on its God and on what God does. It frequently makes the mistake of taking the totality of its own faith for the totality of God. Because of this, religious leaders of Jesus' day made a complete miscalculation. They believed that the death of Jesus on the cross would make an end to his God who seemed to be much more interested in persons in the outer court than in pious believers inside the Temple. They did not reckon with a God who would tear apart the curtain of the Temple to stand with Jesus in his last moment of agony on the cross.

This God in Jesus on the cross is not a new God. This God has always been and will always be the God who stands in the open and takes the side of those who suffer, no matter who they are or where they are from. Of course this God has been and will always be God for Israel and its people, but at the same time has always been and will always be God for all nations and all peoples. The God who caused the temple veil to tear in two is the God who is open to all, even to "pagans and gentiles."

This is why transpositional theology is not only a possibility but a necessity. God is a "transpositional" God. God moves in and out of national frontiers, does away with religious boundaries, and transcends geographical barriers. In the death of Jesus on the cross, God moves out of the Holy of Holies and makes the divine presence fully known in the outer court. From the cross on Golgotha God moves to the "secular" *oikoumene*. What we encounter on that fully exposed hill was a mobile God capable of moving back and forth within creation.

The task of transpositional theology is to seek to meet this God not only in Israel, not only in those western nations nurtured in "Christian" culture, but also in Latin America, Africa, and Asia. As has been mentioned, black theology, feminist theology, and the theology of liberation are forceful expressions of transpositional theology. The theology that wrestles with cultural, historical, and socio-political realities in Asia is of course also a transpositional theology.

Whatever form it may take, transpositional theology never loses sight of Jesus' death on the cross, for it was at the death of Jesus that the curtain of the Temple was torn from top to bottom, the floodgate keeping God from overflowing into unfamiliar territories was forced open, and the Roman soldier at the foot of the cross was moved to confess: "Truly this man was a son of God" (Mk. 15:39; see Mt. 27:54). In making the confession, the pagan soldier already points beyond the cross to the resurrection.

CHAPTER FIVE

From the Cross to the Resurrection

From Good Friday to Easter Sunday, from the cross to the resurrection, from death to life—what an enormous transposition this is! The gulf between them seems infinitely wide and frighteningly deep. It separates the finite from the infinite, the temporal from the eternal. It seems a vast primordial darkness that swallows up everything that makes life and history possible. It seems a negation of the meaningful.

But something impossible happened. Two days later, the disciples were gripped by the astonishing experience of Jesus' resurrection, an experience that transformed them, changed completely their attitude toward the cross, and decisively altered their understanding of the life and ministry of Jesus. Resurrection, this power of transformation, creates hope in the despairing heart. It brings the light of life into the darkness of death. And above all, it creates a new faith powerful enough to generate a vision of God at work redemptively in the life and history of humankind.

Resurrection is the anchor, so to speak, of the New Testament. A New Testament without the resurrection would be like a ship cut loose from its anchor, drifting away aimlessly in the vast ocean. The story of Jesus would have ended on Golgotha. It would have been just another tragedy in the history of human struggle for national and political self-fulfillment.

But the resurrection did take place. The New Testament did get written on the basis of the experience of and witness to the resurrection of Jesus. No wonder there is substantial agreement among New Testament scholars that the resurrection played the predominant role in the writing of the narrations and accounts collected in the New Testament. Werner Kümmel, a German New Testament theologian, for instance, puts it this way:

This understanding of the Jesus tradition growing out of the belief in the resurrected One not only led to the penetration into the Jesus tradi-

97

tion of the confession of Jesus as the Son of God. Above all, the Christians strove to understand the most puzzling event of Jesus' life, his death on the cross, in terms of God's will.[1]

In other words, resurrection is the key to the interpretation of the message of the New Testament. The great disruption caused by the cross is now taken up into the resurrection. The cross moves into the resurrection, giving rise to a faith that bears witness to God's saving love in the world.

RESURRECTION—THE DECISIVE ENLIGHTENMENT

The Christian faith is, first and foremost, a resurrection faith. Jürgen Moltmann, a German theologian, puts it well when he says:

> Christianity stands or falls with the reality of the raising of Jesus from the dead by God. In the New Testament there is no faith that does not start *a priori* with the resurrection of Jesus.[2]

The resurrection of Jesus, or the experience of it, is the foundation stone of faith in the New Testament. Removing this foundation, the house called the New Testament would collapse. Among the writers of the New Testament the one who most passionately expresses this pivotal nature of the resurrection for the Christian faith is St. Paul. He puts it emphatically:

> . . . if Christ was not raised, then our gospel is null and void, and so is your faith; and we turn out to be lying witnesses for God, because we bore witness that he raised Christ to life [1 Cor. 15:14–15].

St. Paul's argument here is very clear. What makes the gospel true and our faith authentic is the resurrection of Jesus. Should the resurrection of Jesus turn out to be untrue, the gospel would at once become untrue and our faith would also become unauthentic.

It was the same with Peter. In his sermon on the day of Pentecost in Jerusalem, Peter proved himself to be a bold preacher full of vivid images and allusions to a cosmic catastrophe on the day of judgment. There was nothing unique in this, for it was the favorite theme of prophets and apocalyptic seers. What made his preaching refreshingly different and decisive was his proclamation of the resurrection of Jesus. "Men of Israel, listen to me," he declared:

> The Jesus we speak of has been raised by God, as we can all bear witness. Exalted thus with God's right hand, he received the Holy Spirit from the Father, as was promised, and all that you now see and hear flows from him [Acts 2:32–33].

It was this message of resurrection that marked that particular Pentecost off from all the other Pentecosts in the past. It was this resurrection faith that led Peter and his fellow apostles to a deeper insight into God's saving will manifested in Jesus Christ. And in a radical reorientation in relation to the life and ministry of Jesus through their experience of the risen Christ, they became the first witnesses to the gospel rejected by the Jewish religious authorities.

The resurrection of Jesus must have been to them a liberating experience. It liberated them from the weight of their religious and cultural traditions. It also enabled them to overcome the understanding of Jesus solely in terms of their socio-political aspirations.

All in all, it led them to a radically new situation where their pre-understanding of Jesus had to give way to understanding him as a post-resurrection event. The experience of the risen Christ was their enlightenment, to use a Buddhist term—that is, an occasion that enabled them to grasp Jesus as the savior not conditioned by Jewish national and religious interests.

The disciples' enlightenment was very decisive. In fact, it was so decisive that Jesus now appeared to them in a completely new light. We must therefore explore the nature of this enlightenment. We must ask what is the power that came to them in their experience of the risen Christ. We must look for the sources on which they drew for their ministry in the post-Easter days.

THE PROFOUND EMPTINESS OF THE TOMB

There is first of all the empty tomb. What makes the new orientation of faith so dramatic is of course not the tomb, but the *emptiness* of the tomb. From the death on the cross to the tomb there is a logical movement. When it became clear that the crucifixion was inevitable, those who had sided with Jesus openly or privately must have begun to prepare for his burial. Joseph of Arimathea, "a man of means" (Mt. 27:57), "a respected member" of the Sanhedrin (Mk. 15:43), "a good, upright man" (Lk. 23:50), "a disciple of Jesus, but a secret disciple for fear of the Jews" (Jn. 19:38), offered "his own unused tomb" (Mt. 27:59). Nicodemus, also a member of the Jewish Council, who must have followed Jesus with a mixture of admiration and caution since that night Jesus conversed with him about being born of the spirit (Jn. 3:1-15), joined with Joseph of Arimathea and others in getting ready for Jesus' entombment (Jn. 19:39).

There was not the slightest question that the cross must be followed by the tomb. Entombment was to be the final act in that whole series of tragic happenings from Jesus' arrest to his crucifixion. It would seal forever this tragic episode in the history of resistance movements against foreign political powers.

Thus, when Mary of Magdala went to visit the tomb on the Sunday morning after the burial, she expected to catch another, perhaps last, glimpse of Jesus' body in the tomb. It never occurred to her to expect something extraordinary. She was astonished when she saw that the heavy stone blocking the entrance to the tomb had been moved away. Utterly confused and worried, she concluded that someone must have come the previous night to remove Jesus' body. She lost no time in reporting this to "Simon Peter and the other disciple, the one whom Jesus loved" (Jn. 20:2). This was the beginning of the drama that was to change fundamentally the image of Jesus in the disciples and early believers.

Because an empty tomb is such an unnatural thing, beyond human comprehension, reaction to the account of Mary of Magdala ranges from incredulity to surprise. Luke put it most aptly when he said that "the story appeared to them [the apostles] to be nonsense, and they would not believe them" (24:11). Even Peter, chief of the disciples, the first to enter the tomb following Mary's report, "went home amazed at what had happened" (24:11). Perhaps it was Thomas who vocalized most candidly the doubt deep in the hearts of many when he said heatedly: "Unless I see the mark of the nails on his hands, unless I put my finger into the place where the nails were, and my hand into his side, I will not believe it" (Jn. 20:25).

All this shows, at the outset at least, that the empty tomb must have presented to the disciples and other followers of Jesus a much greater dilemma than did the cross. The process that led to the cross was in a sense comprehensible, but the empty tomb destroyed the logic of life and death, contradicted the law of nature, and disrupted the continuity of historical experience.

Indeed, the resurrection of Jesus completed the great disruption in history caused by the cross. A profound emptiness was now created in the historical consciousness of Jesus' followers brought up in Jewish religio-political traditions. The history of the Jewish nation, through Jesus' disciples and through those who had welcomed him as an expected messiah, pursued Jesus to the depth of agony on the cross. But that history had to come to a halt at the door of the emptiness of Jesus' tomb. Even the formidable power of faith combined with the political aspiration to bring into being a new messianic nation could not remove that emptiness. It was there to stay in the history of the Jewish people.

That emptiness symbolizes once again the fact that the saving work of God in the world cannot be explained totally by the history of Israel. But this was not all there was in that emptiness, for from that emptiness a new life and a new history were to come into being. It was thus not an *empty* emptiness. On the contrary, it was a *full* emptiness. What kind of emptiness could this be?

The emptiness of the tomb must have been a divine pause in the history of Israel—a pause that God took to prepare the disciples of Jesus for a radical reorientation of their life and faith. The history of Israel from the exodus down to the time of Jesus had been a nonstop history of wars. It was a history filled with both excitements and disappointments—excitements at times of success and victory, disappointments at times of failure and defeat. This history of excitements and disappointments culminated on the cross. And after the cross, the Jewish nation as a whole, including Jesus' followers, were prepared to pick up their history again where it left off, continuing their pursuit of a messianic kingdom. That is why there had to be a pause—a pause to drive home to the followers of Jesus that they could not continue their business as usual, that their history could not go on as if nothing had happened, and that the salvation of the world could not depend solely on reestablishing Israel as a messianic nation.

In the tomb of Jesus the history of Israel was confronted with an impenetrable emptiness. The history of Israel bypassed it, and it was left to the disciples and apostles to face it in order to venture into a new course of history. This is partly the reason why St. Paul turned to the gentiles, having failed to get his fellow Jews to accept the cross and the resurrection of Jesus as the decisive turning point in the history of their nation. The fullness of that emptiness has now to be demonstrated in what God has been doing among the nations. This seems to be the main burden of St. Paul's arguments in chapters nine and ten of his Letter to the Romans.

The emptiness of Jesus' tomb is also a divine space in world history—a space that God created to enable nations and peoples to find their place in the divine saving love. The human space between the history of Israel and the history of the nations is the space of suspicion, misunderstanding, conflict, and confrontation. It is the space where people of different cultures and religions try to undo one another, to outmaneuver one another, and to shed one another's blood in the name of God. It is the space where God's salvation for some means God's condemnation for others. It is, furthermore, the space in which religious believers surmise God's will in their national and personal interest, and interpret God's saving work in conformity with their traditions and teachings. It is a very restricted space where God's accessibility to people is severely limited.

The divine space created by the emptiness of the tomb replaced such human space. That divine space was emptied of all human logic, for was it not pure nonsense for the dead Jesus to leave his tomb fully alive? That divine space had no room for theological investigation and quibbles, for was it not an offense to religious orthodoxy for the crucified criminal to rise from the dead? All in all, the emptiness of the tomb signifies God's absolute beginning with the world and with history.

In short, the empty tomb is God's time and space, in the light of which life and history must be reevaluated, reinterpreted, and reorganized. Because of the empty tomb, life considered as a process toward death must be challenged, for life is now a movement toward life—not just any life, but life in God. Because of the empty tomb, history ceases to be an arena where one nation conquers another nation, one religion triumphs over another religion. Imbedded in history is God's power to carry history to its fulfillment— fulfillment of God's love for all humanity. Furthermore, because of the empty tomb, the world no longer lies at the mercy of the power of destruction and decay. On the contrary, the world can be renewed and revitalized as witness to God's victory over the power of death and destruction.

The empty tomb was therefore a formidable phenomenon. Confronted with it, the disciples were at first dubious, surprised and even frightened. But as the initial shock yielded to a rekindled faith, the empty tomb became part and parcel of their proclamation of the gospel. Jesus, they began to proclaim, was the Christ they had encountered under the powerful impact of the empty tomb. It was not easy for them to come to the risen Christ from Jesus of Nazareth. But with the empty tomb standing in front of them, they could not but see Jesus of Nazareth in the risen Christ. A hermeneutical transposition from the risen Christ to the crucified Jesus has taken place. The accounts in the Gospels, in Acts, and Paul's letters are vivid testimonies to the life and ministry of Jesus of Nazareth experienced in relation to the risen Christ.

CHRIST IS RISEN!

The empty tomb was followed by the appearance of the risen Christ to the disciples and his followers. This is the next point in our study of resurrection as the key to a transpositional hermeneutic. For our discussion we want to select four accounts that seem to stand out as most significant in relation to transpositional hermeneutic. These four accounts are: the appearance of the risen Christ to Mary of Magdala (Jn. 20:11–18; Mk. 10:9–11; Mt. 28:9–10); to the disciples at Emmaus (Lk. 24:13–35); to the disciples, especially Thomas (Jn. 20:24–29); and to the disciples by the Lake of Tiberias (Jn. 21:1–19).

1. Rabbouni!

The first three accounts of Jesus' appearance to Mary of Magdala, to Thomas, and to the disciples at Emmaus, though the scenarios are not the same, seem to have one common emphasis: historical continuity is not crucial in the recognition of the risen Christ.

Let us take the case of Mary of Magdala. Earlier we noted that she was the first person to reach Jesus' tomb that Sunday morning, only to discover that the huge stone at the entrance of the tomb had been removed. Of course this was not the end of the story. As the excitement at discovering the tomb empty subsided, the garden returned to the quietness normal for that early morning hour. Mary remained unaffected by what had just taken place. She had not yet reached her enlightenment, so to speak. The sight of the empty tomb ("she peered into the empty tomb"—Jn. 20:12), conversation with two angels inside the tomb (20:12–13)—all this did not make Mary *recognize* the "transformed Jesus"[3] when she saw him (20:14).

It was not until the risen Christ called her name that she was suddenly lifted out of her preoccupation with the crucified Jesus and was transposed to the presence of the risen Lord. The calling of "Mary" by the risen Christ elicited from her a brief but strong confession: "Rabbouni!" (20:16)—my Teacher and my Lord!

2. How Dull You Are!

The appearance of the risen Christ to the two disciples on the road to Emmaus is even more illustrative of how recognition of him needs much more than understanding of him in relation to the "messianic" history of Israel. Apparently the report of the resurrection had also reached these two, but it did not seem to lighten their hearts. As they told Jesus about the resurrection as well as the crucifixion, their faces were "full of gloom" (Lk. 24:18). For them the cross was essentially a miscarriage of the national expectation for a liberator. This was what worried them. They said to the risen Christ, among other things: "But we had been hoping that he was the man to liberate Israel" (24:21). Even Jesus' effort to enlighten their minds by referring to the history of Moses and the prophets and to the scriptures about the suffering Messiah (24:25–27) did not open their mind's eye to recognize the risen Christ. "How dull you are!" said the risen Lord (24:25), perhaps with a sigh.

To recognize the stranger as the risen Christ they had to wait until Jesus "broke the bread and offered it to them" (24:30). The breaking of the bread on this occasion, just as calling out the name of Mary in the garden, was the moment of sudden enlightenment for the two disciples. That action of breaking bread, symbolizing the offering of Jesus' body for the entire world, nullified their understanding of the cross in terms of an aborted messiahship. It forced them to suspend their stubborn reliance on the history of their nation in order to reach faith in the risen Christ.

There is indeed no unavoidable route from the kingdoms of Israel and Judah to the resurrection of Jesus. Nor was there a shortcut from the conventional understanding of the scriptures to the empty tomb. As Jesus pointedly said to the Jews who held the observance of the Sabbath far more important than giving a hand to the helpless: "You study the scriptures diligently, supposing that in having them you have eternal life; although their testimony points to me, you refuse to come to me for that life" (Jn. 5:39). What a tragic irony this is! The Jews plotted to have Jesus crucified on the basis of the arguments derived from the scriptures that were testimonies to him!

The blindness of the two disciples to the risen Christ on the way to Emmaus calls into question the stereotyped understanding of Israel and, for that matter, of Christianity as a messianic community possessing the exclusive access to the secret of God's salvation. The risen Christ was an anomaly to the history of Israel. All the references to the history of Israel and all the arguments from the scriptures did not enlighten the disciples on the reality of the risen Christ.

The resurrection of Jesus has exposed the limitation and weakness of the continuity of a particular history and religiosity as the paradigm to explain God's saving work in the world.

3. My Lord and My God!

The encounter of Thomas with the risen Christ is filled with human quality. Thomas refused to believe the report on Jesus' resurrection and asserted strongly: "Unless I see the mark of the nails on his hands, unless I put my finger into the place where the nails were, and my hand into his side, I will not believe it" (Jn. 20:25). For Thomas the resurrection of the dead Jesus contradicted reason and offended common sense. He therefore asked for physical evidence, believing that none could be given. But when the opportunity presented itself, he, instead of probing the risen Christ with his finger, responded spontaneously with a great confession of faith: "My Lord and my God!" (20:28). What Thomas wanted initially was a physical continuity between the crucified Jesus and the risen Christ. But faith in the crucified *and* risen Christ could not be the outcome of such continuity, for "if Thomas had accepted Jesus' invitation to examine and touch him, Thomas would not have been a believer."[4]

What Thomas, in order to verify the report on Jesus' resurrection, was looking for was a "bodily" connection between the crucified Jesus and the risen Christ. That is why he wanted to "put his finger into the place where the nails were and his hand into Jesus' side." He could have had what he wanted, because the risen Christ offered himself to him. If he had carried out a "physical" examination of the risen Christ, he might have been able to satisfy his reason and allay his doubt, but he would not have been able to enunciate that great confession of faith in the risen Lord. For faith in the risen Christ, physical continuity between the crucified Jesus and the risen Christ is not important; as a matter of fact it can be a hindrance.

The risen Christ asks us not to base our faith in him on what we regard as reasonable, correct, intelligible, or normal. He himself has risen from the dead. An absolute break has occurred in the world that conditions our body, mind, heart, and spirit. Thomas earlier spoke and acted as if such a break had not taken place. He wanted to evaluate the risen Christ in terms of his past experience. He sought to probe the risen Lord through the history and tradition he had grown up with. He did not realize that the risen Christ demands new bases for evaluating life, world, and history. In fact, Christ himself is that new basis. He is the new reality in the light of which old realities must be reappraised. He is also the new reality through which a vision of the future must be sought.

4. It Is the Lord!

This brings us to Jesus' appearance to his disciples at the Lake of Tiberias, the fourth and last story we need to consider here. In some contrast to the three appearances we have just discussed, excitement over sudden recognition of the risen Christ is not a characteristic of this story. Perhaps this has to do with the darkness of the night in which the appearance took place. Even the voice of "the disciple whom Jesus loved" saying "It is the Lord!" (Jn. 21:7) seems to become absorbed into the thick darkness. All one could hear was the ripples of the sea water and heavy breath of the disciples pulling the overloaded fishing net. And against the gray sky and the dark water the risen Lord stood on the shore in a blurred silhouette. Movements of persons, their worries and concerns, their hopes and aspirations, were not so conspicuous. They became blended with nature, forming a harmony in quiet affirmation of the resurrection of the crucified Jesus.

The big catch of fish, reminiscent of the catch that preceded the call of the first disciples (Lk. 5:1-11), was then followed by a quiet breakfast prepared by the risen Christ. Silence in the presence of the risen Lord was too precious to break. It was a silence that was more eloquent than a loud confession of faith, more expressive than frantic gestures of loyalty. It was in that silence that the conversation between the risen Christ and the subdued Peter took place. The conversation did not break the silence; it flowed as a matter of course from it. Nor did it disturb nature just wakening from its night's rest. Rather the conversation accompanied nature opening up to welcome a new day and a new future.

The conversation is concentrated on loving the risen Christ. Loving the risen Christ is a special kind of loving. It differs, for one thing, from loving Jesus in the prospect of national liberation. Peter and his fellow disciples did love Jesus for this cause. They were disappointed, however. They fled when Jesus was sentenced to death on the cross. No, one cannot love Jesus for a cause, no matter how noble or how exalted it may be. Jesus is more than just an instrument for a human cause, even a religious cause. We do not love him, for example, for the sake of the welfare of the Christian church.

The church in the Middle Ages loved him for its own sake. It put its own interest over and above him. It conditioned and shaped him in accordance with its tastes and convenience. It did not love Jesus "more than all else" (Jn. 21:15).

Nor are we to love Jesus for the sake of the purity of Christian doctrine. Theologians tend to be more interested in their "correct" knowledge of God than in God. They seem to be so busy with their "right" interpretation of Jesus that they are in danger of losing sight of Jesus himself. Even when churches, particularly those churches in western Europe, are half empty, they still go about their business as if God depended on their defense of "pure" doctrines for saving the world. They seem incapable of loving Jesus "more than all else."

Loving the risen Christ is different from loving him on the proviso that he takes our side. Peter and some other disciples followed Jesus perhaps because they thought that he was taking their side. And it did look that way. They were poor fishermen and Jesus had many harsh words to say about the rich.

"A rich man," said Jesus, "will find it hard to enter the kingdom of Heaven. I repeat, it is easier for a camel to pass through the eye of a needle than for a rich man to enter the kingdom of God" (Mt. 19:24). Jesus also did speak for the religiously underprivileged over against the religious authorities. He reserved his sharpest criticisms for the Pharisees and scribes when he heaped words of abuse upon them, calling them "hypocrites, blind fools, snakes, and vipers' brood" (see Mt. 23). He seemed to go even further when he identified himself with his politically oppressed compatriots under the Roman rule. When he was told that King Herod was seeking to kill him, he dared to say: "Go and tell that fox . . ." (Lk. 13:31–32). Yes, Jesus does take sides, but the side he takes may not be our side. This must have been partly what the risen Lord meant when he asked Peter: "Do you love *me*?"

In the course of its long history, the Christian church has frequently defended its side as God's side. But it has also seen its side demolished again and again as the wrong side by the forces at work both inside and outside the church. In the sixteenth century the Reformation boldly challenged the pretension of the Roman papacy as the sole channel of God's salvation. The Enlightenment in the eighteenth century proved that reason could be put to good use even if it might pose a threat to the church that had the final say about faith and morals. And needless to say, in the light of scientific discoveries and technological developments in modern times, many of the views on life and the world held by the church in the past as inviolable appear very absurd.

In our own days churches in many parts of the world are often accused of taking the side of the politically and economically powerful—the side of the oppressor. In difficult socio-political situations, the oppressor's side is far easier to take than God's side. But a church inevitably loses its credibility when it opts for the easy side. God's side is almost without exception a difficult side, but in discerning it and identifying with it, a church gives the right answer to the question put by the risen Christ to Peter by the Lake of Tiberias in that distant past: "Do you love *me*?"

In that very oriental setting and atmosphere of disciples sitting around their revered teacher and master, the risen Christ carried the conversation to a depth unknown to Peter and his companions before. "Feed my lambs and tend my sheep," said Christ (Jn. 21:15–17). The lambs and sheep of the risen Christ—are they not the people of God in a wider sense? Peter "receives the charge to feed Christ's flock, old and young alike, lambs as well as sheep. For Christian love must express itself in service even for the least of Christ's brethren."[5]

Love for the risen Christ must now take form among those for whom Jesus came to suffer and die. That love should go beyond the inner circle of believers. With the rising of Jesus from the dead, the horizon of our experience and understanding of God's love must be broadened. God's love cannot be held as a privilege for a few. The God who vindicated the cross through resurrection has initiated a new era for all his people. The risen Christ directs

Peter and the other disciples to a wider world, to "the least of his brethren."

Peter and his fellow disciples must have been awed by this commission given to them by the risen Christ on that quiet morning at the Lake of Tiberias. Every word Christ said must have created an echo in their inner being. Every breath he breathed must have gone into them as a new life-force. The circle of the flock the risen Lord put into their charge was to grow and expand "in Jerusalem, all over Judea and Samaria, and away to the ends of the earth" (Acts 1:8). This commission of the risen Christ must have enabled them to see their post-resurrection mission of witness linked up with Jesus' pre-resurrection mission of suffering. In this risen Christ they finally encountered the suffering messiah.

CHAPTER SIX

The Suffering Messiah

What is absurd to Greeks and offensive to Jews (1 Cor. 1:18) has become the main focus of the faith inspired by the risen Christ. "Suffering messiah" is an absurd notion for the highly cultured Greeks. A messiah conceived within the city-state of Athens, which could boast of one of the most sophisticated political systems in the ancient world, must be a sage-king full of wisdom, power, and glory. He must be a ruler who thrives on the sweat and blood of slaves. He must preside over a society of philosophers and thinkers who have leisure to cogitate, to argue, and to dream because most of the rest of the population had to toil and labor. Moreover, he has to have military prowess, leading his armies into battle, conquering enemy territories, and enslaving captives. His messiahship must be built on and consolidated by his capacity to make others suffer, prostrate before him, and writhe in agony.

Emperors in ancient China, the notorious Shih Huang Ti most of all, "the Fist Emperor" of the Ch'in dynasty (221–206 B.C.), turned out, in most cases, to be no more than such messiahs. Pharaohs in ancient Egypt were no better. And are there any self-styled political messiahs in totalitarian and pseudo-democratic nations in the world today who have not gained their power at the great cost of the lives and freedom of their people?

No one therefore is surprised when Greeks dismissed Jesus the suffering messiah as absurd. By becoming the suffering messiah, Jesus breaks with the elitist political culture that defends and serves the powerful ruling class and exploits the masses of powerless "plebeians." The transposition of Jesus from a political messiah to the suffering messiah is thus of decisive importance. Jesus as the suffering messiah becomes the prototype of "little suffering messiahs" throughout human history. He becomes embodied in the suffering messiahs of the suffering people of Israel, in Egypt, in France, in the United States, in China, in Brazil.

As to the Jews, "suffering messiah" is an offensive notion. Their religious systems and theological sensitivity have set their messiah on a high pedestal of holiness and glory. The messiah they praise and worship has to be free from the contamination of the world. He must be separated from all that is "profane." That is what "sacred" or "holy" means.¹ In fact all religions try to outdo one another in keeping their deity holy and separated from its ordinary worshippers. Temples must be guarded not only by religious personnel but also by spirits and animals. Care must be taken to have a sacred aura surround the deity, keeping out pollution by its mundane devotees and by this impure world. The name of the deity cannot even be mentioned with impunity. Deity becomes *tabu* to the people.

A HIGH-VOLTAGE GOD

Tabu, whose verbal form *tapui* means "to make holy," according to van der Leeuw, a Dutch phenomenologist of religion, "is a sort of warning: 'Danger! High Voltage!' Power has been stored up, and we must be on our guard. The *tabu* is the expressly authenticated condition of being replete with power, and man's reaction to it should rest on a clear recognition of being this potent fullness, should maintain the proper distance and secure protection."² It is this dangerous and high-voltage God with whom the people of the Old Testament had to contend. The Israelites at the foot of Mount Sinai were solemnly warned "not to force their way through to the Lord to see him, or many of them will perish" (Ex. 19:21). They were thoroughly frightened and pleaded with Moses to be the spokesperson for them before God. They were afraid that "if God speaks to us, we shall die" (Ex. 20:19). The God of Sinai is a highly charged deity, a dangerous God. The people could not dream of getting near their God unharmed.

Another dramatic example of a high-voltage God is that of the ark. One would have thought that the ark of God should have occupied a very intimate place in the life and worship of the people. The ark shared their long, hard life in the desert. It guided their way. It brought them victory. All their hopes and dreams concentrated on the ark of God. Their tie with it could not have been closer. They should have been able to touch it, caress it, even embrace it, for it was their life, their hope, and their history.

But when King David decided to move the ark of God from Kiriathjearim to Jerusalem for a permanent settlement, something terrible happened (1 Chr. 13:5-14). As the procession reached the threshing floor of Kidron, the oxen of the cart bearing the ark stumbled. Uzza, one of the two men assigned to guide the cart, instinctively put out his hand to steady the ark, but "the Lord was angry with Uzza and struck him down" (13:10). What a high-voltage ark it was! This happened despite the fact that the procession was accompanied by cheerful singing and by an orchestra of harps, lutes, tambourines, cymbals, and trumpets (10:6). The austerity of God, however, was not mitigated by all this.

Predictably, King David was very much annoyed. He said: "How can I harbor the Ark of God after this?" (10:12) It was too dangerous to have it in the middle of his city. He had it carried to the house of one called Obed-edom, to wait for it to be less charged with fearful power and deadly danger.

As the heir to the religion of the Old Testament, Judaism is a very high-voltage religion. The God of Judaism is carefully protected from unworthy men and women polluted with cares of this world. Persons in the street are unclean because the niceties of religious laws and rituals are just too remote from their daily lives. This God is even more remote from the pagans who have no pious blood, not even a drop of it, in their veins. They are thoroughly contaminated by sins and impiety. To all these persons the God of Judaism is a very dangerous God. They can only try to imagine what that God looks like from the outer court of the Temple. It is this high-voltage religion that Jesus dared to challenge. In the end Jesus was "electrocuted" by that high-voltage religion.

Its faith derived from the Old Testament as well as from the New Testament, Christianity has often proved itself a high-voltage religion too. In the Constantinian era it began to be charged with high-voltage church power reinforced by state power. Its voltage went up higher and higher as time went on until even dukes, princes, and emperors stood in awe of God and of church authorities. As to the poor ignorant persons who lived at the mercy of state and church, they literally had no choice but to let the church decide their fate and submit to a God of judgment. Christianity was a dangerous religion. Persons could appear before its dangerous God only in fear and trembling, mediated by the princes and priests of the church.

Theology developed within a church defending the dangerous God tends to be a high-voltage theology. It provides the church with theological grounds for anathema and excommunication administered to those recalcitrant souls who want to bring God away from ecclesiastical protection and let the world have a better look at God. Mission theology too has been, on the whole, a militant theology that defends God from pagan gods and draws a clear line between salvation and damnation. It is a very highly charged theology from which very few pagans could get away scot-free.

What we see here in the history of religions is a strange union between high-voltage religion and high-voltage socio-political powers. In his study of kingship in the ancient Near East, Mowinckel, a Scandinavian Old Testament scholar, expresses it in this way: "In Mesopotamia the king always retained this close and distinct relation to the deity; and the conception of this relationship was moulded by theological ideas about kingship. Kingship in Mesopotamia was a sacral institution; and the king shared the holiness of the institution to such an extent that we are justified in speaking of his divinity."[3]

If this was true of ancient Mesopotamia, it was also true of ancient China, whose emperors were installed as "Sons of Heaven" invested with heavenly mandate.[4] In Japan too, from ancient times until very recently, emperors were believed to be direct descendants of gods endowed with divine power and authority to rule the nation of the rising sun. In this way, religious and political powers often combine to conspire against powerless peoples and victimize them.

THE GOLD-CROWNED JESUS

One of the most powerful voices in our time protesting against this con-
spiracy of "holiness" is that of the Korean Roman Catholic poet Kim Chi Ha,
tortured and imprisoned for his fight for human rights and democracy in
South Korea. His three-act play "The Gold-crowned Jesus" is set in a "ghetto
in a small Korean city." Leper, Beggar, and Prostitute, the three main characters in the play, are obvious victims of the "political stability and economic
prosperity" created by the powerful rulers. An old priest, well-meaning but
unwilling to upset the truce with the state authorities, refuses to stand out and
speak for the victims. It is left to a defenseless nun to cast her lot with them.
As these helpless creatures endure cold days and unfriendly nights with empty
stomach and injured humanity, the play moves tragically to the third and
final act with a dreary song sung by Leper intoxicated with self-pity and
human insults:

> There is no native earth
> There is no place to rest your tired bodies
> There is no place even for a grave
>> In the heart of winter
>> I have been abandoned
>> I have been abandoned.

> Endless winter
> Darkness of the abyss that I cannot bear
> This tragic time and tide
> This endless, endless poverty
> This empty, cold world
>> I cannot bear it any longer.[5]

As Leper catches sight of the concrete, gold-crowned Jesus pietà nearby, his
self-pity turns into anger. He bursts out: "Sell your Jesus and take your
goodies forever and ever, if you want, I don't care. It's none of my business.
What could there ever be between that concrete Jesus and me? (repeats spit-
ting gesture)."[6]

As it turns out, there is a lot to do between him and the concrete Jesus. To
Leper's profound surprise, Jesus the savior wants Leper to save him from his
concrete encasement. Leper cannot believe his ears when he hears Jesus say:

> I have been closed up in this stone for a long, long time, . . . entombed
> in this dark, lonely, suffocating prison. I have longed to talk with you,
> the kind and poor people like yourself, and share your sufferings. I
> can't begin to tell you how long I have waited for this day. . . this day

when I would be freed and burn again as a flame inside you, inside the very depths of your misery. But now you have finally come. And because you have come close to me I can speak now. You are my rescuer.[7]

The church has alienated Jesus from the people, dressed him up in golden splendor, hoisted him high above the altar in that awe-inspiring chancel, and sealed his mouth with solemn liturgies and eloquent sermons. He has been the captive savior of the captive church.

This Jesus now tells Leper that he must rescue him from his captivity. He must first regain his own freedom before he will be able to bestow freedom on others. He must first recover his power in order to empower those who have no power. Priests, bishops, rich business entrepreneurs, industrialists, not to say powerful rulers, will not of course free Jesus. It falls on Leper, Beggar, and Prostitute to save the savior. A perverse Christology, is it not? But what a penetrating Christology this is when one thinks of Christ rendered immobile by church traditions, ecclesiastical hierarchies, rigid theologies, and sociopolitical forces!

Jesus has not much time to lose. At his urging, Leper finally approaches him and proceeds to free him from his concrete encasement. At that moment the priest, representing the interests of the church, the company president, personifying national economic development, and the policeman, standing for state power, appear on the scene. They exclaim:

Priest:	Aah, the crown of Jesus.
Company President:	Aah, my gold crown.
Policeman:	Aah, the thief!

Then frantic scrambles follow. "The POLICEMAN snatches the crown from the leper, the COMPANY PRESIDENT snatches it from the policeman, and the PRIEST snatches it from the company president. In an instant, the gold crown is returned to the head of Jesus, who grows as stiff as he had been before." Their hopes shattered, Prostitute, Leper and the Nun call out in great anguish: "No! No! No!" As the curtain is lowered, the lights go down and out; darkness descends on the ghetto.[8]

THE SUFFERING MESSIAH

This is the suffering messiah whom many, many persons encounter and embrace from this side of the resurrection. This must also be the suffering messiah whom the disciples of Jesus finally came to recognize and proclaim after their meeting with the risen Christ. Faith in the risen Lord has led them to understand why Jesus refused to be crowned as a national leader who would lead his people to political victory. They now see clearly why Jesus rejected the temptation of a glorious kingship that would have involved demonstrating miraculous powers and bowing to the satanic powers of this world.

The power of kingship is a dangerously high-voltage power. It is corruptible. And the more it corrupts, the more dangerous it becomes. It becomes dangerous to a powerless people. It proclaims martial law; it increases prison populations; it creates widows and orphans. That power muzzles an entire nation; it also tries to muzzle God.

In fact it is relatively easy to become a political messiah by holding out false promises in plenty to a people in despair. He would promise them plenty to eat, safe streets to walk in, a peaceful life to lead. He would even promise that prisons would be emptied and secret arrests would cease. But the power he holds is often incapable of keeping such promises. Very soon citizens will find that each person is a potential political prisoner, that state dungeons brim over with persons suspected of treason, and that lies are forced down their throats as inviolable truth.

The risen Lord with the scars of the nails and spear still on his body must have made his disciples understand that what the world needs most is his example of a suffering messiah. Peter, as he listened attentively to the new commission of love from the risen Lord at the Lake of Tiberias, must have felt ashamed of having tried to dissuade Jesus from the cross at that moment of excitement in Caesarea Philippi. He must have felt irritated and angered at himself that Jesus had had to say to him sternly: "Away with you, Satan; you are a stumbling block to me. You think as men think, not as God thinks" (Mt. 16:23).

The world looks for political messiahs and is ready to hand over to them power and authority to rule over it. But God looks for suffering messiahs. No, God does not only look for them, but becomes the suffering messiah in Jesus Christ. It eventually dawned on the disciples that only the suffering messiah can promise a new future and give a new life through his cross and resurrection. It is only the suffering messiah who keeps the light of truth, love, and justice shining in the bleak world of lies, extortion, and hatred. It is only the suffering messiah who bears sufferings in the world and brings courage, strength, and hope to those who live in the fear of darkness and the shadow of death. And it is this suffering messiah who makes room and space in the hearts of men and women for God and for one another. The gospel that the disciples left behind them is the gospel of the suffering messiah, not a political messiah.

If the world cannot be helped by a political messiah, it gets no help either from a religiously institutionalized messiah. This is another decisive element that the post-Easter experience brought to the disciples. Jesus is a suffering messiah rejected by a religious messianism consolidated on the long established premises of political and cultural nationalism.

Joachim Jeremias, a German New Testament scholar, has made, it seems, a conclusive analysis of the disciples' understanding of Jesus' suffering before and after the Easter experience. According to him, the accounts of Jesus' breaking the Sabbath on a number of occasions, his cleansing of the Temple, and the pronouncements of his own suffering (e.g., Mk. 14:8; Lk. 13:32) were by no means formulated *ex eventu.*[9] They have to do with what happened during Jesus' ministry. The disciples, preoccupied with a messiah nationally and politically oriented, did not understand these events in relation to Jesus as a suffering messiah. As Jeremias observes, "Despite the tendency of the tradition to spare the disciples, the context repeatedly brings out their lack of understanding and their failure."[10]

Their almost grotesque misunderstanding of Jesus' messiahship is typified in the story of James and John, the sons of Zebedee, who came to Jesus with the request that they be given positions of honor and power in Jesus' kingdom (Mk. 10:35-40; Mt. 20:20-23). This incident shows "how the disciples are wrapped up in expectations of glory which pass over the suffering ahead."[11] These are, however, the bad old pre-Easter days.

The Easter experience has brought about a fundamental change. Jeremias cites the three passion predictions in Mark 8:31 (Mt. 16:21; Lk. 9:22), 9:31 (Mt. 17:21; Lk. 9:44) and 10:33-34 (Mt. 20:18-19; Lk. 18:32-33) as constructed *ex eventu.* The sequence of events related to Jesus' suffering in these passages and especially in its most detailed form in Mark 10:33-34 "corresponds," says Jeremias, "so exactly with the course of the passion narrative and the Easter story, even down to details, that there can be no doubt that this passion prediction is a summary of the passion formulated after the event."[12] The Easter experience did open up for the disciples and the small community of faith surrounding them a radically different dimension of Jesus' messiahship—suffering.

What is of great importance to note is that it is through suffering that the messiahship of Jesus gets linked up with the servanthood of the prophet depicted so majestically in the "Servant Songs" in Second Isaiah, particularly in chapter 53. This is not all. The disciples in the post-Easter community begin to cast their eyes anew on the long history and traditions of their nation and to reinterpret it with the suffering of the messiah in view. In Peter's Pentecostal sermon, the crucified and risen Christ is the main theme to which his account of the history of Israel leads (Acts 2:14-36). Again in his discourse at Solomon's portico later, Peter relates "the God of Abraham, Isaac and Jacob, the God of our fathers and prophets" to "the Messiah who should suffer" (Acts 3:14-36).

When we come to the martyrdom of Stephen, we should note that his last testimony is not a testimony to the history of Israel from Abraham through the exodus to the Davidic dynasty as the working out of God's messianic purpose. Rather, with the last strength and courage he can master, he brings that long and turbulent history of his own nation to the single focus of Jesus. He points to the high priest and his accusers and declares: "And now you have betrayed him and murdered him" (Acts 7:52). For the dying martyr Stephen, Jesus the suffering messiah has become the core of the gospel. A messiah is inconceivable apart from suffering. Suffering is the essence of messianic quality. The pendulum has swung exactly in the opposite direction. A glorious messiah has yielded completely to a suffering messiah.

The thinking of the early community of faith in Jesus as the suffering messiah develops further. In Mark 10:45 we have a most concise theology of suffering messiahship: "For even the Son of Man did not come to be served but to serve, and to give up his life as a ransom for many." Suffering is undergone by the messiah not for his own sake, but for the sake of "many"—that is, for "the countless multitudes."[13] The exclusive understanding of God's salvation is now overcome. God in Jesus Christ is for the Jews, yes, but God is also for the Greeks and barbarians.

As we know, it is St. Paul who stretched this logic of God's saving love to its limit. In his classic statement he is bold enough to say: "There is no such thing as Jew and Greek, slave and freeman, male and female; for you are all one person in Christ Jesus" (Gal. 3:28). St. Paul has replaced the exclusive logic of his own religion with the inclusive logic of God manifested in Jesus Christ.

The suffering of Jesus the messiah has removed all human barriers. It makes God available to human beings and enables them to be part of the divine mystery of salvation. The depths of God's suffering ought to be the place where all persons, despite their different backgrounds and traditions, can recognize one another as fellow pilgrims in need of God's saving power. Religious traditions tend to alienate strangers. Ecclesiastical structures become walls surrounding faithful believers. Doctrinal precision creates heretics and infidels. Even expressions of religious devotion in worship and liturgy make peoples alien to one another.

Suffering, however, does not need to be transmitted by traditions; it is present here and now, as well as in the past. It needs no ecclesiastical sanction; it comes and goes without anyone's bidding. It does not have to be defended doctrinally; it is our daily experience. It cannot be worshipped and adored by fine liturgy; it is to be endured and not to be idolized. To be human is to suffer, and God knows that. That is why God suffers too. Suffering is where God and human beings meet. It is the one place where all persons—kings, priests, paupers, and prostitutes—recognize themselves as frail and transient human beings in need of God's saving love. Suffering brings us closer to God and God closer to us. Suffering, despite all its inhumanity and cruelty, paradoxically enables humans to long for humanity, find it, treasure it, and defend it with all their might.

But what happens so often in the Christian church is that suffering is eulogized and the cross becomes decked with silver and gold. Once suffering is made into a virtue and the cross is decorated with precious stones, the meeting between God and believers becomes a diplomatic ceremony full of pleasantries but devoid of truth. Human encounters turn into a hide-and-seek in which vanity of religion becomes more important than the suffering God in the midst of suffering humanity. When that happens, we lose the ground of communication with God and with one another through God.

That is why the risen Christ has to bring home to the disciples that he is a suffering messiah. Fortunately for the post-Easter disciples, they are able to grasp Jesus as a suffering messiah. They realize that a messiah with a gold crown on his head might save a nation but cannot redeem suffering humanity. And it is humanity in suffering that longs to be taken into the bosom of God laid open in the suffering of Jesus the messiah.

JUSTIFICATION OF THE TAX COLLECTOR

Suffering constitutes Jesus' messiahship. It has fundamentally changed his attitude toward his own religion. Jesus turns to "the countless multitudes" who suffer, while the religious authorities of his time practice a religion for "the few" who are ritually and ethically blameless. Jesus concerns himself almost exclusively with sinners, whereas respectable priests and theologians are almost totally busy with the righteous. With the hindsight of post-Easter insights the disciples must have come to realize fully what Jesus intended when he told the parable of the Pharisee and the tax collector praying in the temple. In this poignant parable,

> The Pharisee stood up and prayed thus: "I thank thee, O God, that I am not like the rest of men—greedy, dishonest, adulterous; or for that matter, like this tax collector. I fast twice a week; I pay tithes on all that I get." But the other kept his distance and would not even raise his eyes to heaven, but beat his breast, saying, "O God, have mercy on me, sinner that I am" [Lk. 18:11–13].

The contrast between the two men is grotesque to the point of being ridiculous. That Jesus draws such a contrast ridiculing the sanctimonious act of prayer is shocking enough. But even more shocking to the ears of his sympathizers and opponents alike, Jesus pronounces that "it was this man—that is, the tax collector—and not the other, who went home acquitted of his sins" (18:13).

Lest anyone should think that Jesus caricatures the established religion of his time by putting that prayer in the Pharisee's mouth, let us be reminded of a first-century prayer of a Pharisee in the Talmud very similar to the one in Jesus' parable. This is the prayer:

> I thank thee, O Lord, my God, that thou hast given me my lot with those who sit in the seat of learning, and not with those who sit at the street corners; for I am early to work, and they are early to work; I am early to work on the words of the Torah, and they are early to work on things of no moment. I weary myself, and they weary themselves; I weary myself and profit thereby, while they weary themselves to no profit. I run and they run; I run towards the life of the Age to Come, and they run towards the pit of destruction.[14]

A model prayer for pious believers, is it not? How can God not accept them with open arms?

But there are in such a prayer some factors that militate against Jesus' understanding of relations between God and human beings. First, the religion expressed in the prayer is the religion of a few selected persons and not of the masses. Those who pray that prayer are proud of the fact that they are in the company of the learned, separated from the rabble in the streets. God hears the prayers of learned believers and appreciates the profound reasoning of theologians. Theirs is an erudite God who demands erudition as an essential part of the practice of faith. Their God is not interested in those ignorant persons who have no deep divine knowledge of God, cannot be bothered with meticulous rituals, and do not know how to order their lives in conformity to the law.

This is not all. The religion demonstrated in such prayer is a religion with "spiritual profit" as its chief concern. It is a profit-oriented religion, looking down upon those who "work on things of no moment" and who "weary themselves to no profit." God for such religion is a profit-conscious God. Such a God has no patience with those hard-pressed people who have to toil for their "material profit" and cannot afford the time for the daily prayers prescribed in their religious handbooks. God has no sympathy for those who worry themselves almost to death because tomorrow holds no promise of food and shelter for them. God is enthroned in the Holy of Holies intent on reaping spiritual profits from the well structured pietism practiced by religious leaders versed in the Torah, in canon law, in doctrine and moral imperatives.

We should notice further that the religion typified in such prayer is a religion directed to the future. A vivid contrast is made here between "life in the age to come" and "life in the pit of destruction." Clearly, the former points to a promising future, while the latter refers to those barred from God's future. God for such religion *is* in the future. God forever beckons from the future. Future is God's essence. Once future becomes the present, God becomes less than God. God guards the future as a life-and-death matter. God must not be grasped in the present. The God we think we have grasped is a mere idol and there is no shortage of such idols—food, shelter, human dignity, a decent life, and so on. That is why God stands in the safe distance of the future, calling us from "the age to come."

But who can really afford such a future? Who has the leisure to be attracted to it? Only those who are well fed, securely sheltered, in command of power, and with riches to spare. The future is the luxury of the rich, the pious, and the powerful. They can afford to think of God in terms of their own future. It is this God of the future that they hold out to the deprived, the poor, the defenseless, the crowds in the streets. Of course they know this is an invitation the masses cannot honor. The fate waiting for them is the pit of destruction outside "the life in the age to come." To all intents and purposes, this is a judicious religion, in which God works out salvation judiciously.

It seems the lot of the masses to suffer at the hand of the judicious God taught by the religious authorities in charge of the masses' "spiritual profit." It is precisely from the tyranny of this lot that Jesus sets out to free humankind for the love and grace of God. This really amounts to declaring that the religion of the few has gone wrong. That kind of religion has falsified God. It has turned God against human beings and alienated them from God. It has made both God and humans victims of its power. By saying that the tax collector went home justified, Jesus exorcises the power of judicious religion, declares the end of the religion of the righteous, and repudiates the piety of the select few. But he does not stop there. He pronounces God's love for the masses. He conveys God's mercy to the crowds in the street and in the marketplace. He comes out into the open to be the savior for sinners.

SAVIOR FOR SINNERS

Jesus has indeed so much to do with sinners that he cannot but offend the religious and moral sensitivity of his religious contemporaries. It is true in general that the more sophisticated a religion becomes, the more refined its sensitivity grows. It elevates to religious sanctity the moral sensitivity created by traditions and defined by its leaders. To offend it is to offend not only spiritual authorities but God. One cannot infringe upon it without serious consequences. This moral-religious sensitivity shields the "sensitive" God from the "insensitive" and uncultured masses.

How the highly privileged Brahmins in India used to treat the outcastes with disdain is well known. The aloofness and sense of superiority with which Confucian literati regarded the uneducated masses are also proverbial.

Is it not also the case that liturgies that have been developed in churches of different confessions and traditions are very much conditioned by moral-religious sensitivity of various kinds? At worship service, particularly in the traditions that put primary emphasis on the mystery of the divine being, moral-religious sensitivity is raised to a high pitch. For many worshipers it must be a relief to leave those highly sensitive moments behind when worship service is over. Jacob expressed it well when that awesome moment of struggling with a "mysterious" person at the ford of Jabbok was over: "I have seen God face to face and my life is spared" (Gen. 32:30). One risks one's life to come to the divine presence. What a sensitive God! What a fearful divine being! And what an awe-inspiring religion!

By turning to sinners and associating with them freely, Jesus has turned his back on such a God, such a divine being, and such an awesome religion. Perhaps we can appreciate more what Jesus is getting himself into if we know what the term "sinner" means in the socio-religious settings of his time. The term means:

(1) People who led an immoral life (e.g. adulterers, swindlers; Luke 18:11) and (2) people who followed a dishonorable calling (i.e. an occupation which notoriously involved immorality or dishonesty), and who

were on that account deprived of civil rights, such as holding office, or bearing witness in legal proceedings, for example, excisemen, tax collectors, shepherds, donkey drivers, peddlers, and tanners.[15]

Sinners are literally social, moral, and religious outcasts. One thing they do not have is respectability. They are subjected to the moral indignation of good citizens. They constantly feel the fingers of religious teachers pointing at their backs. They are, in short, "bad" people excluded from the society and company of "good" people.

Sinners understood in the sense above can be objects of church projects and its outreach in mission. Prostitutes, for example, are objects of church crusades against sins of immorality, and some Christian groups spare no effort to snatch them out of the den of vices, training them to be good members of society. But they cannot easily find warm fellowship within the church. There are alcoholics and drug addicts with trembling limbs and emaciated faces. They are viewed with a mixture of sympathy and annoyance, and churches join in efforts to rehabilitate them. But they are not made to feel at ease in the community of believers immune from such bad habits. There are also offenders of the sanctity of marriage. They are surrounded by gossips in the church and are liable to be disciplined, barred from communion with God and with their fellow Christians at the Lord's table. Those engaged in dubious businesses of one kind or another are of course children of darkness and not children of God.

Churches do have serious concern for sinners such as these, but they are kept at a respectful and cautious distance from the goodly fellowship of faithful believers. From time to time reports of projects on sinners are heard and endorsed in the church. But sinners are not church; they are not among the saved. They are outside the church to keep those inside it busy, to be reminders to them that they are in mission.

But Jesus is not a director of church projects to sinners. He does not behave and act like one, for he brings church to them. He makes sure that if they cannot come to the church, the church must come to them. This should not sound strange, measured by our theological understanding of the relation between Jesus and church. We believe, do we not, that Jesus is the church *par excellence*. Do we not then have to affirm, starting from such belief, that wherever Jesus associates himself with sinners and works with them, there the church is? This is plain logic that no amount of protest on the grounds of piety or theology can refute.

There is a reverse side to this simple logic: when a church refuses to go out to where Jesus is—Jesus who is the church in the true and primary sense of the word—it becomes less than church. God's logic is that simple, but despite its simplicity it is no easy logic. For the Pharisees start accusing Jesus of being "a glutton and a drinker, a friend of tax gatherers and sinners" (Mt. 11:19). Scribes and theologians begin charging him with the deadly sin of being "a blasphemer of God" (Mk. 2:7).

This is an obnoxious twist of God's simple logic of love. Religious leaders and theologians try to beat God at God's own game. They try to convince God that this simple logic is bound to end in self-degradation and self-humiliation, that it would have God blaspheming God, God degrading God, God humiliating God, and God insulting God. In their view, this is precisely what Jesus is doing by resorting to sinners. Ultimately, Jesus means God's suicide. To save God from committing suicide, Jesus must die. This is the logic of church authorities who cannot stand Jesus. The execution of Jesus shows how far human religious logic can go. It does go very far, so far that even God is overtaken by it. On the cross God seems helpless, just as Jesus is. Jesus who mingles with sinners must die like a sinner.

But Jesus is determined to pursue God's logic of love to the end. Nothing seems to deter him from being a friend of sinners and social outcasts. He seeks no religious sanction for his conduct. He invents no theological justification for his conviction. Nor does he appeal to human authority to vindicate himself. This is what he makes absolutely clear: if God is not the God of sinners, then God is not God. If God shuns the company of drunkards, then God is less than God. If God abandons prostitutes, then God is not the creator of all human beings including prostitutes. And if God is afraid openly to show empathy for shady characters, then God is not the redeemer who gives Jesus up as ransom for all.

By stubbornly befriending sinners, Jesus shows that God is God. God cannot deny sinners without denying being God. God cannot reject prostitutes without ceasing to be Immanuel-God with us. God cannot be dissociated from tax collectors without becoming dissociated from God's own self. By turning to sinners in Jesus with resolution and compassion, God decides to be God.

In a most provocative way Jesus reintroduced this God *of* sinners and this God *for* sinners into the religious world of his day. He eats with sinners! In view of the prevailing religious and moral standards, this is an absolutely scandalous thing to do. "It is," says a New Testament commentator, "the aspect of Jesus' ministry which must have been most meaningful to his followers and most offensive to his critics."[16] By eating with sinners, Jesus proclaims in action as well as in words a most startling message: God has no problem with sinners; God accepts them!

There are reasons to believe that Jesus must have felt much more at ease with sinners than with those long-faced practitioners of religion. He attracts sinners to come to him, listen to him and eat with him (Lk. 15:1–2). He invites them to where he was staying and "reclined" at table with them (Mk. 2:15–17). The verb "reclined" (*katakeisthai*) indicates that this is no ordinary meal; it is a festival meal, for the custom was to sit for ordinary meals but to recline for festival meals.[17] The social and religious barriers that exist between the community of the faithful and sinners do not exist between Jesus and sinners.

Why did Jesus' table fellowship with sinners cause such a commotion, such a resentment, within the religious establishment? Why did his eating with them present such an offense to the Jewish authorities? The crux of the matter lies in the profound meaning associated with sharing meals with others. As Joachim Jeremias observes:

> To understand what Jesus was doing in eating with "sinners," it is important to realize that in the east, even today, to invite a man to a meal was an honor. It was an offer of peace, trust, brotherhood and forgiveness; in short, sharing a table meant sharing life.[18]

Sharing a table is a deeply spiritual experience. Eating together is indeed a sacramental act.

First of all, honor is involved in an invitation to a meal. This element of honor tends to make table fellowship a fellowship of discrimination. Since honor is involved, you do not invite just anybody to a meal, not to say to a feast. The more important the occasion, the more selective the list of invitees. To be invited, you have to belong to a certain class—fellowship at a meal is a class fellowship. You have to be a member of a certain society, be it religious, intellectual, professional, or whatever—table fellowship is a societal fellowship. You will also have to have merit of one kind or another, such as wealth, learning, reputation, achievement—eating in fellowship with others is a meritorious fellowship.

Honor associated with table fellowship is thus a conditional honor. It is the honor bestowed on you by your class, your society, or your merit. It is not handed out free of charge; it has to be earned. It is an honor that separates, alienates, and discriminates.

By eating with sinners, Jesus completely upsets the religious and social conventions of honor. Sinners belong to no class, but Jesus gives them class. They are not regarded as members of society, but Jesus recognizes their place in society. They are not in possession of any kind of merit, but Jesus affirms their merit, their *human* merit—that is, the merit given to them by God and not to be taken away on account of their "sins." As they receive Jesus' invitation to a meal and to a feast, they receive from him at the same time honor without charge, an honor without conditions of class, society, or merits. At the table fellowship with Jesus and reclining with him at a feast, they are no longer tax collectors, prostitutes, swindlers, or peddlers; they are *human* beings just as others, embraced by the saving love of God.

THE EUCHARIST IN CHRIST

This is Jesus' evangelism, his acting out of the evangel, *euangelion*. How different it is from churchly evangelism! Evangelism has always been regarded as the central task of the church. The church in evangelism is the church in mission. But do we know of any church that dares to invite prostitutes to a meal within its four walls? Have we seen a church that invites "bad" characters to the Lord's table?

The Lord's table in the church has become such a sacrosanct institution that even "noncommunicant" members are excluded from it, not to say questionable characters. Some historical churches have gone even further. They do not allow Christians of different confessional persuasions to get near to their communion table! The Orthodox, the Roman Catholic, and the Protestant, each church fortifies its own communion table with canon laws, sacramental theology, and ecclesiastical barriers in order to guard its purity and sanctity. But the frightening thought here is that the communion table so fiercely and jealously guarded may turn out not to be the *Lord's* table after all, but merely the church's own table.

There is some basis to this frightening thought, for the communion table ecclesiastically institutionalized seems very remote from the sacramental meals Jesus used to have with sinners. We tend to forget that it is precisely in the context of Jesus' table fellowship with sinners leading to the Last Supper on the eve of his crucifixion that the Lord's table is to be understood and shared. This is essentially what Jeremias means when he writes:

> These gatherings at table, which provoked such scandal because Jesus excluded no one from them, even open sinners, and which thus expressed the heart of his message, were types of the feast to come in the time of salvation (Mk. 2:18–20). The last supper has its historical roots in this chain of gatherings.[19]

Is this not a terribly disturbing thought for the theology and celebration of the eucharist in most churches, Orthodox, Roman Catholic and Protestant? Does this not call into question those theologies of the sacrament that do not express "the heart of Jesus' message"—Jesus' acceptance of all and everyone without exception to his sacramental meals, Jesus' holding feasts even with sinners as "types of the feast to come in the time of salvation"? Our sacrament of the eucharist surely has its historical roots in the traditions of the church. But does it have its historical roots also in the table fellowship Jesus had with sinners and outcasts? This is a critical question.

The theology of the sacrament of the eucharist in the traditional thinking of the church deals with every aspect of the eucharist except this "heart of Jesus' message." It does not face the fact that Jesus accepted everyone, even open sinners. The eucharist has become an institution of salvation in which the "chosen" participate *on behalf of* the rest of humanity but not *with* them. The eucharist has become a "representative" sacrament at which communicant members of the church receive God's blessings for themselves and *for,* but not *with,* people not qualified in the church's view.

One of the recent ecumenical statements on the eucharist makes this evident:

> The eucharist is the great sacrifice of praise by which the Church speaks on behalf of the whole creation. For the world which God has recon-

ciled to himself is present at every eucharist: in the bread and wine, in the persons of the faithful, and in the prayers they offer for themselves and for all men and women. As the faithful and their prayers are united in the Person of our Lord and to his intercession, they are transfigured and accepted. Thus the eucharist reveals to the world what it must become.[20]

A beautiful theological statement! But do we find in it echoes of the joy and gratitude audible and visible at Jesus' table fellowship with sinners? Does it put the eucharist in the setting of the rough and tumble of this world? Theological emphasis on the "on behalf" nature of the eucharistic community in the statement strengthens in fact the isolation of the church from the world. The church becomes a colony of God's salvation established in the world. The expansion of the church is the expansion of this colony of saved believers.

It is perhaps partly for this reason that the churches in the West in the heyday of their missionary outreach did not consider it strange that Christian colonization of the Third World should go hand in hand with the political colonization of the Third World by western powers.

The statement quoted above compels us to ask a further question: does the eucharist as practiced in the churches in history and especially today "reveal to the world what it must become"? The eucharist that has lost touch with its historical roots in Jesus' fellowship with everyone without exception and particularly with "open sinners," the eucharist that ceases to be a sacramental meal *with* all people, the eucharist that has become shrouded in the mystery of church traditions and tangled in canon laws and theological debates, and the eucharist that has become the place where the division of churches becomes painfully visible and real—can such a eucharist reveal to the world what it must become?

The eucharist as an ecclesiastical institution has become the center of the liturgical life of the church severed from the richness and perplexity of life in its totality. It has become a sharing of a spiritual life that conforms to the regulations and rules of respective churches. It offers peace, trust, and forgiveness to the Christian believers who have satisfied the requirements of church authorities.

The honor extended to them by the invitation to the eucharist is a conditional honor. Because it is a conditional honor, sharing of life at the communion table cannot but be a conditional sharing. That is why it has been so difficult to break the barriers that separate Christians of different confessional traditions. That is also why it has become one of the most abstruse aspects of the life and ministry of the church, incomprehensible to those outside the church.

The situation has become completely reversed. When Jesus sat at table with sinners, religious authorities were totally scandalized. That kind of sacramental fellowship was to them a *scandalon,* an offense. But now the eucharist appears to be a *scandalon* not to church authorities but to sinners outside the eucharistic community. The eucharist has become *descandalized* insofar as the church is concerned, but *rescandalized* in relation to those who have no access to it.

Does this not make it imperative to reconstruct a theology of the eucharist starting from the place where it should begin—Jesus' table fellowship with sinners and outcasts? Do we not have to go back to these historical roots for the reshaping of our sacramental theology and of our theology of the church? Should we not consider this an essential part of our obedience to Jesus Christ, the Lord of the eucharist and the Lord of the church?

THE TABLE OF LIFE AND LOVE

Sharing table fellowship means sharing life—this is in essence the mission of God in Jesus. At the center of God's mission is this table of life. This table can be set anywhere—in a home, in front of a house, on a roadside, at a street corner, in a marketplace, in a prison, in a refugee camp. What comes first is the life that the table fellowship can support, cultivate, empower, and affirm. Each table fellowship Jesus has with sinners is the table of communion in love, power, and life. It is the table of God's love, the table of God's power, the table of God's life. And because the table is God's, it becomes ours. It becomes the table of our love, the table of our power, the table of our life. Eating at table with Jesus is at once the most divine and the most human thing. For at table God and human beings meet in Jesus. There at table sinners are touched and embraced by God, and God is felt and moved by sinners.

The story of the woman who dampened Jesus' feet with her tears, wiped them with her hair, and anointed them with ointment is the drama of how God and sinful human beings are moved to mutual embrace in Jesus Christ. The story that Luke tells (7:36–50) is far richer and deeper in meaning than that told by Matthew (26:6–13) or Mark (14:3–9).

In Matthew and Mark, the incident took place at Bethany in the house of Simon the leper. Its setting is that of Passover and the burial of Jesus. Further, the conversation, in their version, between Jesus and his disciples on the woman's anointing him with expensive ointment took on a moralistic tone related to the poor.

The Lukan version is quite different, however. There is nothing moralistic about it. It seems chiefly concerned with the message that God in Jesus is the savior for sinners.

Besides Jesus, the chief actors in the story are a Pharisee called Simon and a woman who, in all probability, is a prostitute (she is described as a sinner, *hamartolos,* in Lk. 7:37). The contrast between the two persons cannot be more striking—the contrast we have been highlighting in our discussion. The Pharisee represents of course all the correctness of religious piety. He stands for religious and moral authority. He is surrounded by an aura of goodness and righteousness. He symbolizes the hope of salvation for believers. In contrast, the woman, as prostitute, is a nobody. She is a shame to society and an offense to piety. Despite such a huge contrast, Jesus draws them together to himself.

The stage for this curious rendezvous is a banquet (*kateklithe* in 7:36) held by the Pharisee in honor of Jesus. It must have been a special feast, for a special honor is involved. Simon the Pharisee may be betting on "the possibility that Jesus may be a prophet, and that with him the departed Spirit of God has returned, bringing the New Age."[21] For Simon the host the banquet must have represented a deeply religious investment. He must have felt strangely restless, for it could be that he is hosting the messiah promised and awaited in the long tradition of his faith. He must have secretly wondered whether this would be a messianic banquet.

The intrusion of the woman, not just an ordinary woman, but a prostitute, into the banquet must have caused Simon the Pharisee extreme dismay. She brings dishonor not only to Simon the host, to his respectable guests, but also to Jesus, the possible messiah. Murmurs of consternation and whispers of displeasure must have begun to fill the room.

The woman in question seems entirely oblivious to all this. She seems completely preoccupied with a single idea—to unburden herself at the feet of Jesus. So concentrated is she in her thought and movement that no one is able to stop her in time. As soon as she finds her place and sits down at Jesus' feet, she begins to weep. She even commits the disgrace of untying her hair in the full view of these men in order to wipe Jesus' feet she has dampened with her tears.

By this time all the guests present and even Simon the host have faded off stage. The drama is now totally focused on Jesus and this sinful woman. These two personalities loom distinct, tender, and in complete harmony in the limelight of God's saving love. It is this love that led her to Jesus in the first place. And it is this love that makes her forget all about social and religious taboos, all about her sinful self, about the shameful way in which she has to earn her living. As she proceeds to anoint Jesus' feet with the myrrh that she has brought along, the fragrance of God's saving love surrounds and embraces her. It fills the entire air, if not the hearts of Simon the Pharisee and his guests.

This is the quality of God's love that radiates from Jesus. It is the quality that attracts sinners and repels the self-righteous. It is the quality that makes you forget your sins and gives you back your human dignity. And above all, it is the quality that makes you long for God.

The heart of God's mission in Jesus is revealed completely when Jesus addresses himself to the reproachful Simon:

> I came to your house: you provided no water for my feet; but this woman has made my feet wet with her tears and wiped them with her hair. You gave me no kiss; but she has been kissing my feet ever since I came in. You did not anoint my head with oil; but she has anointed my

feet with myrrh. And so, I tell you, her great love proves that her many sins have been forgiven; where little has been forgiven, little love is shown [7:44–47].

The heart of God is the heart of love. To be saved is to be embraced by this love. To become healthy is to become enveloped in this love. And it is those who are saved and made healthy in this way who know how to accept other fellow sinners, converse with them, and eat with them.

Between Jesus and the woman a table of life is set up. It is the table of the woman's tears and Jesus' compassion. It is the table at which Jesus shares completely her life of sorrow, guilt, and forsakenness: Jesus accepts her. It is also the table at which the woman shares completely Jesus' life of love, suffering, and sacrifice: she anoints Jesus with oil. The two lives meet at this table of fellowship of life and love. These two lives originated in God and find each other again in God at that table of God's saving love.

This table makes the splendid banquet of the Pharisee look dingy. It robs the gaily decorated banquet room of all its glory and beauty. It renders the guests clothed in honor and dignity shameful and superficial. In this way and only in this way God's love becomes judgmental. It judges so that the loveless may become love-full. It judges in order that those who cannot forgive may be able to forgive. And it judges in the hope that we may always remember that God loves us not because we are sinless but because we are sinful. God's love is our redemptive remembrance. To remember it is to be saved and forgiven. In Jesus God decisively turns to sinners. This makes the communion table the Lord's table and the church the body of Christ.